国家工业遗产

National Industrial Heritage

（第三批）

(The Third Batches)

汉英对照

中国工业报社 ◎ 主编

电子工业出版社

Publishing House of Electronics Industry

北京·BEIJING

内容简介

本书全面展现了工业和信息化部认定的国家工业遗产（第三批）的遗产历史、核心物项、人物故事等珍贵资料，还包含了遗产项目在转型发展、业态重构以及助力城市更新等方面的经验和做法，可为各地进一步促进工业文化产业创新发展提供参考借鉴。全书为中英文双语呈现，颇具研究和收藏价值。

未经许可，不得以任何方式复制或抄袭本书之部分或全部内容。
版权所有，侵权必究。

图书在版编目（CIP）数据

国家工业遗产．第三批：汉英对照 / 中国工业报社主编．—北京：电子工业出版社，2021.8
ISBN 978-7-121-40921-9

Ⅰ．①国… Ⅱ．①中… Ⅲ．①工业企业－企业文化－中国－画册 Ⅳ．① F425-64

中国版本图书馆 CIP 数据核字（2021）第 058897 号

责任编辑：朱雨萌　　文字编辑：邓茗幻
印　　刷：北京利丰雅高长城印刷有限公司
装　　订：北京利丰雅高长城印刷有限公司
出版发行：电子工业出版社
　　　　　北京市海淀区万寿路 173 信箱　邮编：100036
开　　本：880×1 230　1/12　印张：25　字数：435 千字
版　　次：2021 年 8 月第 1 版
印　　次：2021 年 8 月第 1 次印刷
定　　价：398.00 元

凡所购买电子工业出版社图书有缺损问题者，请向购买书店调换。若书店售缺，请与本社发行部联系，联系及邮购电话：（010）88254888、88258888。
质量投诉请发电子邮件至 zlts@phei.com.cn，盗版侵权举报请发电子邮件至 dbqq@phei.com.cn。
本书咨询联系方式：（010）88254750。

编委会

主　　任：徐金宝

编　　委：温舜方　孙　星　周　岚　程　楠　马雨墨

主　　编：郑春蕾

副 主 编：孙　静

编　　辑：贾志佳　张　楠　郭　莹

参编人员：林　玲　高　峰　吴丹远　许绍文　陈新彬　尹　杰　蒋　敏　栾希亭
　　　　　谢燕华　钟连盛　赵元书　何　清　陈保军　曹　鹏　王海龙　徐　委
　　　　　韩　东　汪哲涵　杨永忠　李国龙　李　琼　汤　敏　章燕飞　周美洪
　　　　　周　健　白光华　丁　文　王传勇　毕爱平　黎　阳　夏　敏　胡忠相
　　　　　贺华仲　陈　涛　王相星　袁成方　谢建国　迟恩波　粟才全　王　飞
　　　　　黄小波　陈　勇　尼玉斌　赵晓辉　周　军　张　滢　张　敏　徐新新
　　　　　王　刚　江　仲　刘兴福

Chairman: Xu Jinbao

Editorial Board Member: Wen Shunfang　Sun Xing　Zhou Lan　Cheng Nan　Ma Yumo

Editor-in-Chief: Zheng Chunlei

Associate Editor: Sun Jing

Editor: Jia Zhijia　Zhang Nan　Guo Ying

Participating Staff: Lin Ling　Gao Feng　Wu Danyuan　Xu Shaowen　Chen Xinbin　Yin Jie　Jiang Min
　　　　　Luan Xiting　Xie Yanhua　Zhong Liansheng　Zhao Yuanshu　He Qing　Chen Baojun
　　　　　Cao Peng　Wang Hailong　Xu Wei　Han Dong　Wang Zhehan　Yang Yongzhong
　　　　　Li Guolong　Li Qiong　Tang Min　Zhang Yanfei　Zhou Meihong　Zhou Jian
　　　　　Bai Guanghua　Ding Wen　Wang Chuanyong　Bi Aiping　Li Yang　Xia Min
　　　　　Hu Zhongxiang　He Huazhong　Chen Tao　Wang Xiangxing　Yuan Chengfang
　　　　　Xie Jianguo　Chi Enbo　Su Caiquan　Wang Fei　Huang Xiaobo　Chen Yong　Ni Yubin
　　　　　Zhao Xiaohui　Zhou Jun　Zhang Ying　Zhang Min　Xu Xinxin　Wang Gang
　　　　　Jiang Zhong　Liu Xingfu

前言

大国泱泱，浩浩汤汤，工业文明，源远流长。商周铸铜，秦汉炼铁；酿酒制盐，亘古无双；丝绸瓷器，精美绝伦；军工岁月，淬火华章；飞天入海，烈焰成器；文化传承，复我华邦！

工业乃强国之本，文化是民族之魂。习近平总书记在党的十九大报告中指出："文化是一个国家、一个民族的灵魂。文化兴国运兴，文化强民族强。没有高度的文化自信，没有文化的繁荣兴盛，就没有中华民族伟大复兴。"弘扬优秀工业文化、传承工业精神，是建设制造强国不可或缺的重要组成部分。

新中国成立以来，在中国共产党领导下，我国建立了完整的工业体系，在不同阶段孕育了大庆精神、"两弹一星"精神、载人航天精神、探月精神等辉映时代的工业精神。

工业遗产是工业文化和精神的重要载体。我国在各时期形成的工业遗产蕴含着丰富的经济价值和社会价值，是发展新业态、创造新动力、拓展新空间的独特资源。为加强工业遗产保护和利用，2016年，工业和信息化部印发《关于推进工业文化发展的指导意见》；2020年，工业和信息化部会同国家发展改革委等五部门印发《推动老工业城市工业遗产保护利用实施方案》，对工业遗产保护利用的重要意义、总体要求、主要任务、组织实施等提出要求。

2017—2019年，工业和信息化部组织认定了3批共102项国家工业遗产，并出台《国家工业遗产管理暂行办法》，对工业遗产的认定程序、保护管理、利用发展等予以规定。此项工作抢救性地保护了一批重要工业遗产，引导各地提高活化利用水平，将工业遗产保护利用与城市转型发展相结合，得到社会各方广泛认可与好评。

为了更好地展现工业遗产风貌和文化内涵，受工业和信息化部委托，中国工业报社等单位在汇编出版《国家工业遗产（第一、二批）》画册图书并取得良好反响的基础上，又对第三批国家工业遗产的典型案例与先进经验予以汇编。《国家工业遗产（第三批）》画册图书，不仅含有大量遗产历史、核心物项、人物故事等珍贵资料，还包含了遗产项目在转型发展、业态重构以及助力城市更新等方面的经验和做法，希望能为各地进一步促进工业文化产业创新发展提供参考与借鉴。

编委会
2020年12月

Preface

Our great country, with a long history of industrial civilization, goes forward vigorously. Copper-casting dated back to Shang and Zhou dynasties; iron-making started from Qin and Han dynasties; wine-brewing and salt-making were ancient unparalleled scenery; silk and porcelain were exquisite beyond compare; military years left the country with beautiful prose; crafts and devices were invented into space and sea; with its culture inherited and passed on, China can regain its former glory.

Industry is the base of a great country, and culture is the soul of a nation. "Culture is a country and nation's soul," General Secretary Xi Jinping said in a report to the 19th National Congress of the Communist Party of China. "Our country will thrive only if our culture thrives, and our nation will be strong only if our culture is strong. Without full confidence in our culture, without a rich and prosperous culture, the Chinese nation will not be able to rejuvenate itself. " Promoting excellent industrial culture and inheriting industrial spirit areindispensable parts of building a manufacturing power.

Since the founding of New China, under the leadership of the Communist Party of China, China has established a complete industrial system. From different stages come Daqing spirit, "two bombs and one satellite" spirit, manned spaceflight spirit, lunar exploration spirit and other industrial spirits of the times.

Industrial heritage is an important carrier of industrial culture and spirit. Formed in various periods, China's industrial heritage containsrich economic and social values, and is a unique resource for developing new business forms, creating new driving forces and expanding new space.In order to strengthen the protection and utilization of industrial heritage, the Ministry of Industry and Information Technology issued Guidance on Promoting the Development of Industrial Culture in 2016.In 2020,the Ministry of Industry and Information Technology and the National Development and Reform Commission and other five departmentsissued the Implementation Program for the Promotion of the Protection and Utilization of Industrial Heritage in Old Industrial Cities. In the document were written thesignificance, overall requirements, major tasks and organization and implementation of industrial heritage protection and utilization.

From 2017 to 2019, the Ministry of Industry and Information Technology organized and identified three batches of 102 national industrial heritage, and issued Interim Measures for the Administration of National Industrial Heritage, which stipulated the identification procedures, protection management, utilization and development of industrial heritage.This work has protected a number of important industrial heritage sites, improved the level of activation and utilization in various places, and combined the protection and utilization of industrial heritages with urban transformation and development, which has been widely recognized and praised by all sides of the society.

In order to better display the style and cultural connotations of the industrial heritage, entrusted by the Ministry of Industry and Information Technology, China Industry News Agency and other units collected and compiled typical cases and advanced experience of the third batch of national industrial heritage after the good response of compilation and publication ofNational Industrial Heritage (the First and the Second Batches).The National Industrial Heritage (the Third Batch), not only includes a large number of heritage history, core items, and industrial figures and stories, but also contains the transformation and development, business reconstruction and urban renewal experience and practices, hoping to provide reference for further promoting the innovation and development of industrial culture industry in verious regions.

Committee
December 2020

国家工业遗产管理暂行办法

第一章 总则

第一条 为推动工业遗产保护利用，发展工业文化，根据《中共中央办公厅 国务院办公厅关于实施中华优秀传统文化传承发展工程的意见》《国务院办公厅关于推进城区老工业区搬迁改造的指导意见》，以及《工业和信息化部 财政部关于推进工业文化发展的指导意见》，制定本办法。

第二条 开展国家工业遗产保护利用及相关管理工作，适用本办法。

第三条 本办法所称国家工业遗产，是指在中国工业长期发展进程中形成的，具有较高的历史价值、科技价值、社会价值和艺术价值，经工业和信息化部认定的工业遗存。

国家工业遗产核心物项是指代表国家工业遗产主要特征的物质遗存和非物质遗存。物质遗存包括作坊、车间、厂房、管理和科研场所、矿区等生产储运设施，以及与之相关的生活设施和生产工具、机器设备、产品、档案等；非物质遗存包括生产工艺知识、管理制度、企业文化等。

第四条 开展国家工业遗产保护利用管理工作，应当发挥遗产所有权人的主体作用，坚持政府引导、社会参与，保护优先、合理利用，动态传承、可持续发展的原则。

第五条 工业和信息化部负责国家工业遗产认定等管理工作，指导地方和企业开展工业遗产保护利用工作。

省级工业和信息化主管部门、中央企业公司总部负责组织本行政区域内或本企业国家工业遗产的申报、推荐工作，协助工业和信息化部对国家工业遗产保护利用工作进行监督管理。

第六条 鼓励和支持公民、法人和社会机构通过科研、科普、教育、捐赠、公益活动、设立基金等多种方式参与国家工业遗产保护利用工作。

第二章 认定程序

第七条 申请国家工业遗产，需工业特色鲜明，并具备以下条件：

（一）在中国历史或行业历史上有标志性意义，见证了本行业在世界或中国的发端、对中国历史或世界历史有重要影响、与中国社会变革或重要历史事件及人物密切相关；

（二）工业生产技术重大变革具有代表性，反映某行业、地域或某个历史时期的技术创新、技术突破，对后续科技发展产生重要影响；

（三）具备丰富的工业文化内涵，对当时社会经济和文化发展有较强的影响力，反映了同时期社会风貌，在社会公众中拥有广泛认同；

（四）其规划、设计、工程代表特定历史时期或地域的风貌特色，对工业美学产生重要影响；

（五）具备良好的保护和利用工作基础。

第八条　由遗产所有权人提出申请，经所在地县级或市级人民政府同意，通过省级工业和信息化主管部门初审后报工业和信息化部；中央企业直接向公司总部提出申请，由公司总部初审后报工业和信息化部。

遗产项目涉及多个所有权人的，应协商一致后联合提出申请。

第九条　遗产所有权人应当按要求提交书面申请，同时提交以下文件、材料（复印件）：

（一）遗产产权证明；

（二）图片、图纸、档案、影像资料；

（三）管理制度和措施；

（四）保护与利用规划；

（五）其他可以证明遗产价值的文件、材料。

上述材料内容均不得涉及国家秘密。

第十条　工业和信息化部组织专家对申请项目进行评审和现场核查，经审查合格并公示后，公布国家工业遗产名单并授牌。

第三章 保护管理

第十一条　国家工业遗产所有权人应当在遗产区域内醒目位置设立标志，内容包括遗产的名称、标识、认定机构名称、认定时间和相关说明。国家工业遗产标识由工业和信息化部发布。

第十二条　国家工业遗产所有权人应当在遗产区域内设立相应的展陈设施，宣传遗产重要价值、保护理念、历史人文、科技工艺、景观风貌和品牌内涵等。

　　第十三条　鼓励各地方人民政府和省级工业和信息化主管部门将国家工业遗产的保护利用工作纳入相关规划，通过专项资金（基金）等方式支持国家工业遗产的保护利用。

　　第十四条　国家工业遗产所有权人应当设置专门部门或由专人监测遗产的保存状况，划定保护范围，采取有效保护措施，保持遗产格局、结构、样式和风貌特征，确保核心物项不被破坏。遗产格局、结构、样式和风貌特征出现较大改变的应当及时恢复，核心物项如有损毁的应当及时修复。有关情况应在 30 个工作日内通过省级工业和信息化主管部门或有关中央企业公司总部向工业和信息化部报告。

　　第十五条　国家工业遗产所有权人应当建立完备的遗产档案，记录国家工业遗产的核心物项保护、遗存收集、维护修缮、发展利用、资助支持等情况，收藏相关资料并存档。

　　工业和信息化部负责建立和完善国家工业遗产档案数据库，国家工业遗产所有权人应当予以配合。

　　第十六条　国家工业遗产的核心物项调整按原申请程序提出。

　　第十七条　国家工业遗产所有权人应当按照工业和信息化部的要求，向省级工业和信息化主管部门或有关中央企业公司总部提交遗产保护利用工作年度报告，内容包括当年工作总结、下一年的工作计划、国家工业遗产权属变更和规划调整情况等。

第四章 利用发展

　　第十八条　国家工业遗产的利用，应当符合遗产保护与利用规划要求，充分听取社会公众的意见，科学决策，保持整体风貌，传承工业文化。

　　第十九条　加强对国家工业遗产的宣传报道和传播推广，综合利用互联网、大数据、云计算等高科技手段，开展工业文艺作品创作、展览、科普和爱国主义教育等活动，弘扬工匠精神、劳模精神和企业家精神，促进工业文化繁荣发展。

　　第二十条　支持有条件的地区和企业依托国家工业遗产建设工业博物馆，发掘整理各类遗存，完善工业博物馆的收藏、保护、研究、展示和教育功能。

第二十一条　支持利用国家工业遗产资源，开发具有生产流程体验、历史人文与科普教育、特色产品推广等功能的工业旅游项目，完善基础设施和配套服务，打造具有地域和行业特色的工业旅游线路。

第二十二条　鼓励利用国家工业遗产资源，建设工业文化产业园区、特色小镇（街区）、创新创业基地等，培育工业设计、工艺美术、工业创意等业态。

第二十三条　鼓励强化工业遗产保护利用学术研究，加强工业遗产资源调查，开展专业培训及国内外交流合作，培育支持专业服务机构发展，提升工业遗产保护利用水平和能力，扩大社会影响。

第五章 监督检查

第二十四条　工业和信息化部对国家工业遗产保护利用工作进行指导和监督。省级工业和信息化主管部门、有关中央企业公司总部应根据工业和信息化部要求，组织开展本行政区域内或本企业的国家工业遗产保护情况的检查和评估工作，向工业和信息化部及时报告检查、评估发现的问题。

第二十五条　鼓励社会公众对国家工业遗产保护利用工作进行监督，公众发现国家工业遗产保护利用不符合本办法规定的，可向工业和信息化部反映。

第二十六条　国家工业遗产核心物项损毁并无法修复，不再符合认定条件的，由工业和信息化部将其从国家工业遗产名单中移除，遗产所有权人及有关方面不得继续使用"国家工业遗产"字样和相关标志、标识。

第六章 附则

第二十七条　省级工业和信息化主管部门可结合本地区实际，参照本办法组织开展省级工业遗产的认定和管理工作。

第二十八条　本办法由工业和信息化部负责解释，自发布之日起施行。

目 录

北 京 Beijing
北京珐琅厂 002
Beijing Enamel Factory Co.,Ltd.

度支部印刷局 010
The Printing Bureau of the Board of Appropriation Budge

天 津 Tianjin
大港油田港 5 井 014
Portwell 5, Dagang Oilfield

河 北 Hebei
开滦赵各庄矿 018
Zhaogezhuang Coal Mine in Kailuan

山 西 Shanxi
"刘伯承工厂"旧址 024
Former Site of Liu Bocheng Factory

石圪节煤矿 030
Shigejie Coal Mine

高平丝织印染厂 036
Gaoping Silk Printing and Dyeing Factory

辽 宁 Liaoning
抚顺西露天矿 040
West Open-pit Mine

营口造纸厂 044
Yingkou Paper Mill

大连冷冻机厂铸造工厂 050
Dalian Refrigerator Foundry

黑龙江 Heilongjiang
一重富拉尔基厂区 054
China First Heavy Industries Fulaerji Plant Area

龙江森工桦南森林铁路 060
Huanan Forest Railway of Longjiang Forest Industry

X

上 海 Shanghai

上海造币厂 ········· 066
Shanghai Mint

江 苏 Jiangsu

常州恒源畅厂 ········· 072
Changzhou Heng Yuan Chang Plant

恒顺镇江香醋传统酿造区 ········· 080
Hengshun Zhenjiang Spiced Vinegar Traditional Brewing Area

洋河老窖池群及酿酒作坊 ········· 086
Yanghe Old Pits Group and Wine-making Workshops

浙 江 Zhejiang

绍兴鉴湖黄酒作坊 ········· 092
Shaoxing Jianhu Yellow Rice Wine Workshop

安 徽 Anhui

古井贡酒年份原浆传统酿造区 ········· 098
Traditional Brewing Area of Gujing Tribute Wine Original Pulp

贵池茶厂 ········· 104
Guichi Tea Factory

歙县老胡开文墨厂 ········· 110
Shexian Old Hu Kaiwen Ink Factory

福 建 Fujian

泉州源和堂蜜饯厂 ········· 116
Quanzhou Yuanhetang Candied Fruits Factory

福建红旗机器厂 ········· 122
Fujian Red Flag Machine Factory

江 西 Jiangxi

景德镇明清御窑厂遗址 ········· 128
Jingdezhen Ming-and-Qing Dynasty Imperial Kiln Factory Site

景德镇国营为民瓷厂 ········· 134
Jingdezhen State-run Weimin Porcelain Factory

目 录

吉州窑遗址 140
Jizhou Kiln Site

兴国官田中央兵工厂 146
Xingguo Guantian Central Military Factory

山 东 Shandong

潍坊大英烟公司 152
Weifang Daying Tobacco Company

东阿阿胶厂78号旧址 158
The original site of Dong'e Ejiao Factory No.78

湖 北 Hubei

湖北5133厂 162
5133 Factory of Hubei Province

华新水泥厂旧址 168
Former Site of Huaxin Cement Factory

湖 南 Hunan

中核二七二厂铀水冶纯化生产线及配套工程 172
272 Plant of CNNC Uranium Hydrometallurgy and Purification Production Line and Supporting Projects

广 东 Guangdong

南风古灶 178
Nanfeng Ancient Stove

重 庆 Chongqing

核工业816工程 184
Nuclear Industry—Project 816

重庆长风化工厂 190
Chongqing Changfeng Chemical Plant

四 川 Sichuan

成都水井街酒坊 194
Chengdu Shuijing Street Distillery

自贡井盐 200
Zigong Well Salt

攀枝花钢铁厂 ·· 206
Panzhihua Iron and Steel Works

洞窝水电站 ·· 212
Dongwo Hydroelectric Station

隆昌气矿圣灯山气田旧址 ··· 218
Former Site of Shengdeng Mountain Gas Field in Longchang Gas Mine

核工业受控核聚变实验旧址 ·· 226
Original Site of Controlled Nuclear Fusion Experiment of Nuclear Industry

嘉阳煤矿老矿区 ·· 232
Old Mining Area of Jiayang Coal Mine

贵 州 Guizhou

六枝矿区 ·· 238
Liuzhi Mining Area

贵州万山汞矿 ·· 244
Wanshan Mercury Mine of Guizhou

云 南 Yunnan

云南省凤庆茶厂老厂区 ·· 250
Yunnan Fengqing Tea Old Factory Area

西 藏 Tibet

羊八井地热发电试验设施 ·· 256
Yangbajing Geothermal Power Test Facility

陕 西 Shaanxi

红光沟航天六院旧址 ·· 260
Former Site of the Sixth Research Institute of Hongguanggou Aerospace

中科院国家授时中心蒲城长短波授时台 ··· 266
Pucheng BPL&BPM National Time Service Center of Chinese Academy of Sciences

定边盐场 ·· 272
Dingbian Saltern

甘 肃 Gansu

中核 504 厂 ·· 278
China Nuclear Plant 504

国家工业遗产（第三批）

北京珐琅厂

景泰蓝行业唯一的中华老字号
The Only Time-honored Chinese Brand in the Field of Cloisonne

壹：遗产春秋
Section one: History

北京市珐琅厂有限责任公司前身是北京珐琅厂，成立于1956年，由42家私营珐琅厂和专为皇家制作景泰蓝的造办处合并组成。当时的珐琅厂有12个生产点，分布在王府井、前门、崇文门一带，1957年全厂迁到现在的厂址。1958年，国营特艺实验厂并入珐琅厂，北京珐琅厂更名为国营北京珐琅厂。

Beijing Enamel Factory Co.,Ltd. formerly known as Beijing Enamel Factory, was founded in 1956. It was made up of 42 private enamel factories and the Royal Cloisonne Workshop. Back then the factory has 12 plants distributed in the area of Wangfujing, Qianmen and Chongwenmen. In 1957, all plants were relocated to its current site. In 1958, the State-owned Special Art Experimental Plant was incorporated into the factory, and thereafter it was renamed as the State-owned Beijing Enamel Factory.

年届82岁高龄的国家级非物质文化遗产传承人、中国工艺美术终身成就奖获得者、中国工艺美术大师钱美华先生创作的《和平尊》，从立意构思到制作完成，历时一年多，是为喜迎祖国六十华诞推出的献礼作品，也是收官之作。

Master of Chinese Arts and Crafts Qian Meihua, also entitled the 82-year-old inheritor of National Intangible Cultural Heritage and winner of the Lifetime Achievement Award of Chinese Arts and Crafts, has created "Zun of Peace". It took more than a year from thinking up the idea to completing the handicraft. It is a tribute to celebrate the 60th birthday of the motherland, and also the last work of Master Qian Meihua.

遗产名称/位置：北京珐琅厂/北京市
Heritage item/Location:Beijing Enamel Factory Co., Ltd. / Beijing City

建厂之初，北京珐琅厂就制定了景泰蓝工艺操作规程、各工序质量标准等600多年景泰蓝技艺史上的第一批标准，引导传统手工业从经验转向标准化生产。2002年，北京市珐琅厂改制成立北京市珐琅厂有限责任公司。作为国家非物质文化遗产生产性保护示范基地、景泰蓝行业唯一的中华老字号，北京市珐琅厂具有鲜明的北京地域文化特征、历史痕迹、独特工艺与经营特色，不仅是国内景泰蓝行业保存最为完整的近代工业遗产，更是北京近代轻工业发展的实物见证。

Right after its foundation, the factory established such standards as cloisonne handicraft procedures and quality standards in every procedure, which were the first batch of standards in cloisonne industry over the last 600 years. The establishment of such standards made it possible to pass on the traditional handicrafts by standardized procedures instead of by experience. In 2002, Beijing Enamel Factory was restructured into Beijing Enamel Factory Co., Ltd. As the protected production model base of the National Intangible Cultural Heritag, and the only time-honored Chinese brand in cloisonne industry, Beijing Enamel Factory is boasted with distinctive regional cultural characteristics, historical marks and unique craftsmanship and operation philosophy. It is not only the best preserved domestic cloisonne industrial heritage, but also witness Beijing's modern light industrial development.

阅读链接 Link for further reading

景泰蓝
Cloisonne

景泰蓝，学名铜胎掐丝珐琅，是金属胎嵌搪瓷工艺在中国衍生出的独立品种。其技艺是用铜作胎，将细铜丝轧扁后以手工制成各种图案，掐、焊、贴在胎体上，再施珐琅釉料，经过烧制、磨光、镀金等多道工序最后制作出成品。

Cloisonne, the scientific name is copper enamel, which is evolved in China from metal padding enamel craftsmanship. The first step to make a cloisonne is to weave the flattened copper into different patterns, which are inlaid, welded or attached onto the copper-made base, onto which the enamel glaze is applied. After such processes as burning, polishing and gold plating, a handicraft is completed.

明清两代，御用监和造办处均在北京设有专为皇家服务的珐琅作坊，景泰蓝技艺从成熟走向辉煌，名列"燕京八绝"之一。近代以来，由于社会动荡不安，北京景泰蓝技艺一度衰微。

In Ming and Qing Dynasties, both Royal Ware Office and Royal Workshops set up enamel plants in Beijing. Thus cloisonne crafting skills went from upscale to exquisite, and were included as one of the "Eight Yanjing Wonders". Since modern times, Beijing cloisonne crafting skills have declined due to social unrest.

新中国成立后，国家采取积极的保护、扶持政策，使得这一古老技艺焕发生机。2006年，景泰蓝制作技艺被列入第一批国家级非物质文化遗产。

After the founding of the People's Republic of China, the state adopted an active policy of protection and support, which brought this ancient skill to life. In 2006, cloisonne crafting skills were included in the first batch of National Intangible Cultural Heritage.

北京

贰：核心物项
Section two: Core items

北京珐琅厂工业遗产的核心物项包括原职工食堂；制地机、鳔丝机、手摇梭子机、滚床、烧活大炉及冲压机等机械设备，反映不同时期景泰蓝生产工序（制胎、掐丝、点蓝、烧活）的工具；1956年公私合营原始登记资料、钱美华大师人事档案及设计原稿、珐琅厂老艺人作品拓片等历史档案；景泰蓝制作技艺。

The core items of the industrial heritage of Beijing Enamel Factory include the original staff canteen and equipments as base-modeling machine, wire-inlaying machine, hand-shaking shuttle machine, rolling bed, burning furnace and the stamping machine, reflecting the tools in the production of cloisonne of different periods (base-modeling, wire-inlaying, enamel glazing, fire heating). Other core items are the original public-private partnership registration material in 1956, personnel files of master Qian Meihua and her design manuscripts, historical archives of rubbings of old artists' handicrafts, and cloisonne crafting skills.

20世纪80年代第二生产车间掐丝工序操作场景。
Wire-inlaying operation scene in the second production workshop in the 1980s.

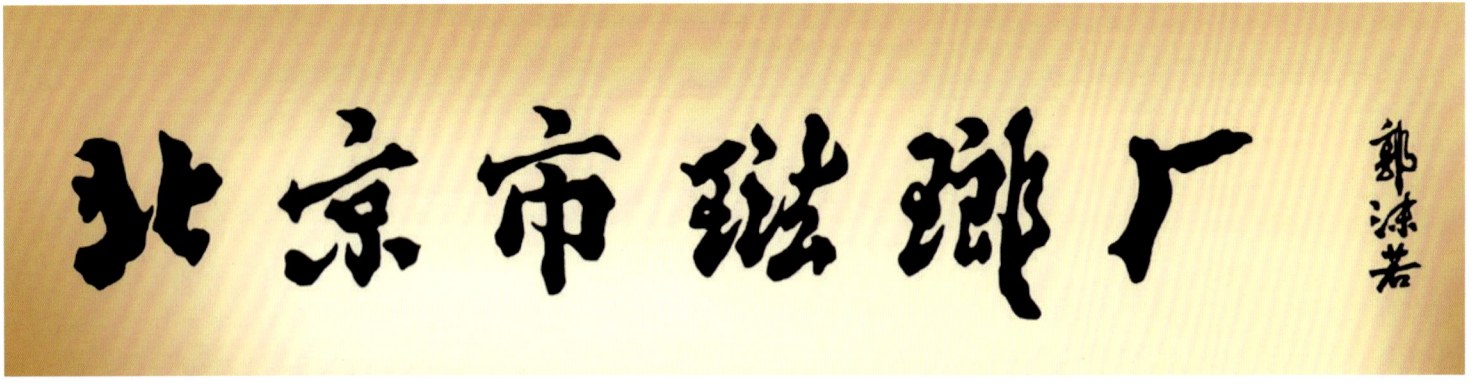

1958年，现代著名文学家、历史学家郭沫若为合并后的北京市珐琅厂题写厂名。
In 1958, Guo Moruo, a famous modern writer and historian, wrote its name in Chinese calligraphy for Beijing Enamel Factory.

遗产名称/位置：北京珐琅厂/北京市
Heritage item/Location:Beijing Enamel Factory Co., Ltd. / Beijing City

北京

烧制40寸以上景泰蓝大瓶采用的大型地坑炉。
Large pit furnace for firing large Cloisonne bottles of more than 40 inches.

制地机、自制压丝机等机械设备。
equipments-as base-modeling machine, factory-made wire-inlaying machine.

钱美华：景泰蓝专业设计第一人
Qian Meihua: Number One in Cloisonne Design

20世纪50年代，就读于中央美术学院华东分院的钱美华，被选送到清华大学营建系深造，师从著名建筑学家梁思成、林徽因，主研工艺美术，抢救濒于灭绝的景泰蓝。

In the 1950s, Qian Meihua, who studied in Huadong College of Central Academy of Fine Arts, was selected to go further study in the Department of Construction at Tsinghua University. There she studied under the famous architects Liang Sicheng and Lin Huiying, majoring in arts and crafts. In this way she begun her journey inheriting the endangered cloisonne crafting skills.

当时，北京仅存的几家作坊和景泰蓝厂大都处于倒闭边缘，新老艺人青黄不接。在林徽因的指导下，美术组为景泰蓝设计了一批具有民族风格的新颖图案，几位当时被迫改行拉黄包车的老技师被请回厂时，都激动得热泪盈眶。

At that time, Beijing's only few workshops and cloisonne factories were mostly on the verge of bankruptcy with fewer veterans and green hands available for the craftsmanship. Under the guidance of Lin Huiying, the design group drew up a number of novel patterns with nationalistic style. Several old technicians who were forced to change their trade to pull rickshaws were excited to tears when invited back to the factory to participate in the undertaking.

20世纪50年代的钱美华与沈从文。
Qian Meihua and Shen Congwen in the 1950s.

遗产名称 / 位置：北京珐琅厂 / 北京市
Heritage item/Location: Beijing Enamel Factory Co., Ltd. / Beijing City

为了解景泰蓝的发展历程，钱美华听取沈从文的建议，去故宫参观临摹珍藏的景泰蓝器物，终于掌握了传统纹样的规律，并编写出我国第一部景泰蓝创作教材《景泰蓝创作设计》。

In order to understand the development history of cloisonne, Qian Meihua consulted Shen Congwen. She went to the Forbidden City to observe and copy conserved cloisonne. Finally she found the law of traditional patterns and thus compiled China's first cloisonne design textbook *Creative Design of Cloisonne*.

钱美华是景泰蓝这一中国传统工艺当代传承的标志性人物，也是新中国知识分子从事景泰蓝专业设计的第一人，对景泰蓝工艺的现代化发展产生了重要影响，并使之得以发扬光大。

Qian Meihua is an iconic figure in the field of contemporary cloisonne inheritance and the first modern intellectual engaging in cloisonne professional design. She has had an important influence on the development and flourish of cloisonne craft.

北京

20世纪80年代钱美华设计的玉兰瓶手稿。
A manuscript of a magnolia bottle designed by Qian Meihua in the 1980s.

20世纪八九十年代钱美华的代表作品福寿周器垒和如意尊。
Qian Meihua's representative works Fushou Zhouqilei and Ruyizun in the 1980s and 1990s.

叁：遗产活化
Section three: Revitalization

利用旧厂房改建的国内首座景泰蓝博物馆开馆，以元、明、清时期制作风格的珐琅器为主，展示了中国景泰蓝技艺的传承与发展。
The first Cloisonne Museum was revamped from its old factory buildings; its main exhibitions are enamel handicrafts with the production style of Yuan, Ming and Qing Dynasties, so as to demonstrate the inheritance and development of China's cloisonne craft skills.

参考资料：《中国工艺美术大师·钱美华：景泰蓝》。
Reference: *Chinese Master of Arts and Crafts · Qian Meihua: Cloisonne.*

景泰蓝博物馆内景。
Interior of cloisonne Museum.

国家工业遗产（第三批）

度支部印刷局

中国第一家官办现代化印钞企业
The First Modern Banknote Printing Enterprise in China

壹：遗产春秋
Section one: History

　　坐落于北京南城白纸坊地区的北京印钞有限公司（以下简称"北钞"）建成于1908年，其前身为清政府度支部印刷局，是中国第一家官办现代化印钞企业，也是中国最早印制邮票的企业。中国第一张采用现代化钢凹版雕刻印刷技术设计印刷的钞票——大清银行兑换券就诞生于此。它在建立之初，从美国引进了当时世界上最为先进的钢凹版雕刻印刷技术和印刷设备，聘请美国著名雕刻技师海趣等人来华设计纸币、传授技艺，印刷局的规模样式则仿照"美京国立印刷局"设计建造。

　　Located in Bai Zhifang area of the southern part of Beijing, Beijing Banknote Printing Co., Ltd. (BBPC) was established in 1908, whose predecessor was The Printing Bureau of the Board of Appropriation Budge of the Qing government. It was the first modern banknote printing enterprise in China. It was the place where the first banknote designed and printed with modern steel intaglio engraving printing in China was born. It was also the earliest enterprise to print stamps in China. At the beginning of its establishment, it introduced the most advanced steel intaglio engraving printing technology and equipment from the United States, and employed eminent American carving technician Lorenzo J. Hatch and others to come to China to design paper money and teach the technique. The scale and style of the Printing Bureau were modeled on the design and construction of the "U.S. national printing office".

　　新中国成立后，北钞在印制战线对国家的金融发展贡献卓著，涌现出一批杰出的科技研发和设计雕刻人员。先后参与过第一套至第五套人民币的设计与印制，为十多个国家和地区印制货币，还设计、印制了人民币第一张塑料钞票——迎接新世纪纪念钞。

　　Since the People's Republic of China was founded, BBPC has made outstanding contributions to the financial development of China in the printing realm, and has fostered a number of outstanding technological researching and design and carving personnel. They have participated in the design and printing of the first to the fifth sets of RMB. What's more, they have printed currency for more than ten countries and regions. Moreover, they also designed and printed the first plastic banknote, Commemorative Note for the New Century.

遗产名称/位置：度支部印刷局/北京市白纸坊
Heritage item/Location: The Printing Bureau of the Board of Appropriation Budge/ Bai Zhifang area of Beijing City

贰：核心物项
Section two: Core items

主工房大楼，钟楼，水塔，专家楼 3 栋；万能雕刻机，单针缩刻机，手扳凹印机。

Main workshop building, bell tower, water tower, 3 expert buildings; universal engraving machine, single needle engraving machine, hand operated gravure printing machine.

北京

办公大楼。工字大楼由美国米拉奔公司设计、日商华胜公司包建土木工程，1910年6月1日动工，1914年秋竣工，建筑面积12 220平方米（五层）。工字大楼于1989年由工房改为办公用房，现为北钞办公大楼。2009年重新进行了室内装修保护。

Office building. The I-shaped building was designed by an American company, Miraben, and constructed by Japanese Huasheng Company. The construction started on June 1st, 1910 and was completed in the autumn of 1914. The building covers 12 220 square meters (five floors). This I-shape building was converted from a workshop into an office building in 1989, and is now the office building of BBPC. In 2009, an interior decoration protection was carried out.

国家工业遗产（第三批）

北钞钟楼正面全景。该钟楼建成于民国四年（1915年）。雪白的廊檐勾勒出青砖墙体，跟其身后的办公大楼和东侧的三座西式小楼造型相近，浑然天成。
Panoramic view of the front of the bell tower of BBPC. The bell tower was built in 1915. The white porch eaves outline the blue brick wall, which is similar to and matches the office building behind it and the three western style buildings on the east.

旧钟楼。
The old bell tower.

遗产名称/位置：度支部印刷局 / 北京市白纸坊
Heritage item/Location: The Printing Bureau of the Board of Appropriation Budge/ Bai Zhifang area of Beijing City

北京

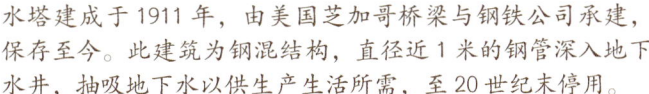

水塔建成于1911年，由美国芝加哥桥梁与钢铁公司承建，保存至今。此建筑为钢混结构，直径近1米的钢管深入地下水井，抽吸地下水以供生产生活所需，至20世纪末停用。

The water tower was built in 1911 by Bridge and Steel Company of Chicago, and has been preserved to this day. The structure of this building is steel-concrete. The steel pipe with a diameter of nearly 1 meter goes deep into the groundwater to pump groundwater for production and living needs, and it worked till the end of the 20th century.

单针缩刻机。
Single needle engraving machine.

手扳凹印机（展陈于中国印钞造币博物馆）。
Hand operated gravure printing machine (exhibited in the Museum of China Banknote Printing and Minting).

国家工业遗产（第三批）

大港油田港 5 井

大港油田第一口发现井
The First Discovery Portwell in Dagang Oilfield

壹：遗产春秋
Section one: History

大港油田港 5 井，坐落于天津市滨海新区大港油田港东地区。该井保护区为东西长南北宽的长方形，占地面积 2 700 平方米。

Portwell 5, Dagang Oilfield, is located in Gangdong area of Dagang Oilfield in Binhai New Area in Tianjin. The protection area of this portwell is a rectangle with east-west length and south-north width, covering an area of 2 700 square meters.

港 5 井是大港油田的第一口发现井、功勋井。该井于 1964 年 11 月 17 日开钻，12 月 20 日，在钻进老第三系沙河街组三段上部约 2 526.34 米时，喜喷高产油气流，证实了大港构造高压油气层的存在，验证了李四光同志对于环渤海湾地区有广阔找油前景的预测。

Portwell 5 is the first discovery portwell and a meritorious portwell in Dagang Oilfield. The portwell started drilling on November 17th, 1964. On December 20th, 1964, it sprayed high-yield oil and gas flow when drilling about 2 526.34 meters in the upper part of the third member of Shahejie formation. The existence of high pressure oil and gas reservoirs in Dagang structure was confirmed, and the prediction of Li Siguang for oil exploration in Bohai Bay area was verified.

天津大港油田港 5 井。
Portwell 5, Dagang Oilfield, Tianjin.

遗产名称/位置：大港油田港 5 井/天津市滨海新区
Heritage item/Location: Portwell 5, Dagang Oilfield/Tianjin City

港 5 井不仅见证了大港油田艰苦奋斗的创业历程，传承了石油精神和大庆精神、铁人精神，更承载了大港石油人保障国家能源安全的铮铮誓言和"我为祖国献石油"的光荣使命。之后，在大港油田的基础上，陆续诞生了华北油田、渤海油田、冀东油田。

Well Gang 5 not only witnessed the pioneering course of Dagang oilfield through hard work, inherited the petroleum spirit, Daqing spirit and iron man spirit, but also carried the solemn oath of Dagang Petroleum people to ensure national energy security and the glorious mission of "I offer oil to the motherland". After that, on the basis of Dagang Oilfield, Huabei Oilfield, Bohai Oilfield and Jidong Oilfield were successively discovered.

天津

历史档案资料：入关打井。
Historical Archives: Drilling Wells into the customs.

贰：核心物项
Section two: Core items

港 5 井；华北石油勘探会战时期用过的钻头及工具箱、管钳和样桶；港 5 井的岩芯；历史档案。
Portwell 5; bits and tool boxes, pipe tongs and sample barrels used during the oil exploration battle in the North China area; core of Portwell 5; historical archives.

历史档案资料：入关打井。
Historical Archives: Drilling Wells into the customs.

遗产名称/位置：大港油田港5井/天津市滨海新区
Heritage item/Location: Portwell 5, Dagang Oilfield/Tianjin City

叁：遗产活化
Section three: Revitalization

目前，大港油田公司严格执行文物遗产相关保护管理制度，并由第一采油厂指定专人负责港5井，每周对港5井设备设施进行日常检查并做好日常维护工作。同时，充分发挥企业精神教育基地功能，目前，港5井每年接待各类参观30余次、千余人次，已成为大港油田公司员工岗位教育、厂史教育、传统教育、党性教育的经常性、永久性基地和对外展示的重要窗口。

At present, Dagang Oilfield Company strictly implements the protection and management system related to cultural relics and heritage, and The First Oil Production Plant designates a special person to be responsible for Portwell 5, and carries out daily inspection and maintenance work on the equipment and facilities of it every week. At the same time, the function of education base of enterprise spirit was given full play. At present, Portwell 5 receives more than 30 visits and more than 1 000 persons a year. It has become an important window for external display, and a regular and permanent education base for on-job training, factory history, traditional education and party spirit education.

港5井的石雕。
Stone carvings of Portwell 5.

国家工业遗产（第三批）

开滦赵各庄矿

百年矿山见证中国煤炭工业变革
A Century of Mine Witnessing the Development and Reform of the Coal Industry of China

壹：遗产春秋
Section one: History

开滦赵各庄矿是由清末民初民族实业家周学熙于1906年创办的一座具有百年历史的煤矿。

Zhaogezhuang Coal Mine in Kailuan is a 100 year old coal mine founded by Zhou Xuexi, a national industrialist in the late Qing Dynasty and the early Republic of China.

1912年开滦赵各庄矿开始修建的铁路，采用蒸汽机车外运煤炭，20世纪二三十年代生产的火车轨道至今仍铺设在地面。

In 1912, Zhaogezhuang Coal Mine in Kailuan began to build a railway, using steam locomotives to transport coal. The railway tracks produced in the 1920s and 1930s are still laid on the ground.

遗产名称/位置：开滦赵各庄矿/河北省唐山市古冶区
Heritage item/Location: Zhaogezhuang Coal Mine in Kailuan/Tangshan city of Hebei Province

110年的蹉跎岁月，开滦赵各庄矿保留了大量上世纪工业遗迹，见证了开滦赵各庄矿发展历程和中国煤炭工业发展变革，是近代煤炭工业发展史的重要标志，积淀了深厚独特的煤炭工业文化。

After 110 years of wasted time, Zhaogezhuang Coal Mine in Kailuan has retained a large number of industrial relics of the last century, witnessed the development process of Zhaogezhuang Coal Mine in Kailuan and the development and reform of China's Coal industry. It is an important symbol of the development history of modern coal industry and has accumulated profound and unique coal industry culture.

贰：核心物项
Section two: Core items

1、2、3、4号井井架；1号井绞车房及内部绞车设备；建矿初期使用的工具及工牌；9、10号洋房子；图纸。

Derricks of No.1, No.2, No.3 and No.4 well; winch house and internal winch equipment of No.1 well; tools and badges used in the initial stage of mine construction; No.9 and No.10 western-style house; drawings.

河北

建矿初期使用的工牌。
Badges used in the initial stage of mine construction.

绞车设备。
Winch equipment.

10号洋房子：晚清末年，清政府筹办开平矿务局时，由英国官方买办兴建的独具特色的西式居所。
No.10 western-style house: a unique western-style house built by the British official comprador when the Qing government launched the Kaiping Mining Bureau in the late Qing Dynasty.

遗产名称/位置：开滦赵各庄矿/河北省唐山市古冶区
Heritage item/Location: Zhaogezhuang Coal Mine in Kailuan/Tangshan city of Hebei Province

河北

1、2、3、4号井井架：1909年2月14日，开滦赵各庄矿动工开凿1、2、3号大井，1910年1月14日正式生产出煤。
Derricks of No.1, No.2, No.3 and No.4 well: On February 14th, 1909, Zhaogezhuang Coal Mine in Kailuan started to dig No.1, No.2 and No.3 well, and the coal was officially produced on January 14th, 1910.

国家工业遗产（第三批）

110年风雨兼程，涌现的典型人物故事，积淀形成了开滦赵各庄矿"顾全大局、百折不挠、敢于为首，追求不渝"的光荣传统和企业精神。

Through 110 years of trials and hardships, typical characters' stories have emerged here, which has formed the glorious tradition and industrial spirit of "take the whole situation into consideration, persistence, dare to lead and pursue unswervingly" of the miners in Zhaogezhuang Coal Mine in Kailuan.

著名的抗日英雄节振国，积极参与开滦五矿同盟大罢工，刀劈鬼子兵、杀汉奸，威震冀东大地，留下了许多可歌可泣的事迹，成为开滦工人阶级的宝贵财富。

Jie Zhenguo, a famous Anti Japanese hero, took an active part in the general strike of Kailuan Minmetals Alliance. He slashed devils and soldiers and killed traitors, which shocked the East of Hebei Province. He left many touching stories and became the precious wealth of Kailuan working class.

李长振，20世纪50年代首创的"单人支柱"操作法，曾在全国煤炭系统广泛推广。1956年以开滦矿工身份参加了中共第八次全国代表大会，受到党和国家领导人的亲切接见，是开滦矿工中最早的全国党代会代表。

Li Changzhen, the first "single pillar" operation method, which was widely promoted in the national coal system in the 1950s. In 1956, he attended the Eighth National Congress of the Communist Party of China as a miner in Kailuan. He was cordially received by the leaders of CPC and the state. He was the earliest representative of the National Party Congress among Kailuan miners.

侯占友，全国著名劳动模范，20世纪70年代，为缓解当时全国煤炭的紧张状况，为了多出煤，他连班加点，不计报酬，经常自带干粮，吃住在井下。1975年5月25日，新华社播发的长篇通讯中，称侯占友为"地球转一圈，他转一圈半，地球转两圈，他上三个班"的"矿山铁汉"。

Hou Zhanyou, a well-known model worker in China, in the 1970s, in order to ease the national coal shortage at that time and to produce more coal, he worked overtime without pay and often brought his own food and lived underground. On May 25th, 1975, the *Xinhua News Agency* broadcast a long news, calling Hou Zhanyou a "mining iron man" with "one and a half circles of the earth, two circles of the earth, and three classes".

节振国雕像。
Statue of Jie Zhenguo.

遗产名称/位置：开滦赵各庄矿/河北省唐山市古冶区
Heritage item/Location: Zhaogezhuang Coal Mine in Kailuan/Tangshan city of Hebei Province

叁：遗产活化
Section three: Revitalization

  为进一步保护开发工业遗产，助推企业转型发展，开滦赵各庄矿深入挖掘整合矿区红色党史资源，致力于开发红色旅游资源，积极打造爱国主义教育基地，充分利用工业建筑遗产及洋房子资源，开发工业旅游及影视拍摄基地，凸显开滦赵各庄矿百年历史价值。

  In order to further protect and develop the industrial heritage and boost the transformation and development of enterprises, Zhaogezhuang Coal Mine in Kailuan deeply excavates and integrates the red party history resources in the mining area, devotes itself to developing red tourism resources, actively builds a patriotism education base, makes full use of industrial architectural heritage and foreign house resources, develops industrial tourism and film and television shooting base, highlighting the 100 year historical value of Zhaogezhuang Coal Mine in Kailuan.

唐山开滦赵各庄矿业有限公司的工业遗产"10号洋房子"外景。
The exterior view of "No. 10 Foreign House", the Industrial Heritage of Tangshan Kailuan Zhaogezhuang Mining Co., Ltd..

河北

国家工业遗产（第三批）

"刘伯承工厂"旧址

刘伯承工厂：军工精神的象征
Liu Bocheng Factory: a Symbol of Military Spirit

壹：遗产春秋
Section one: History

　　1945年11月，兵工二厂（前身是黄崖洞兵工厂）从平顺西安村搬迁到山西省长治市南石槽村，是华北最大的兵工厂，主要产品是82迫击炮弹。

　　In November 1945, the Second Munitions Factory (formerly Huangyadong Munitions Factory), then the largest munitions factory in North China, was moved from Xi'an Village, Pingshun county to Nanshicao Village, Changzhi City, Shanxi Province. 82 mortar shells were its main productions.

刘伯承工厂旧址正门。
The main gate of the former site of Liu Bocheng Factory.

遗产名称/位置："刘伯承工厂"旧址/山西省长治市
Heritage name/Location: Former Site of Liu Bocheng Factory/Changzhi City, Shanxi Province

1947年，"刘邓大军"千里挺进大别山，拉开了解放战争的序幕。为有力支援前线，晋冀鲁豫军区军工处以毛泽东同志提出的工业生产要"数量多、质量好、成本低、原料足、销路广"的生产方针为内容，在所属19个兵工厂中开展"刘伯承工厂"立功竞赛运动。兵工二厂取得了产量高、质量好、技术改革成果大等突出成绩，被晋冀鲁豫军区军工处授予"刘伯承工厂"荣誉称号，并形成了"一切为了前线"的刘伯承工厂精神。现在，刘伯承工厂厂部、生产工房等建筑基本保存完好。

In 1947, Liu Deng's army marched thousands of miles into the Dabie Mountains, opening the prelude of the war of liberation. In order to provide strong support to the front line, the military industry division of the Shanxi Hebei Shandong Henan military region carried out a meritorious competition for "Liu Bocheng Factory" among its 19 subordinate munitions factories, which was based on comrade Mao Zedong's production policy of "large quantity, good quality, low cost, sufficient raw materials and wide market". The Second Munitions Factory, achieved outstanding achievements such as high output, good quality and great achievements in technical reform, and was awarded the honorary title of "Liu Bocheng Factory" by the military industry division and formed the factory spirit of "all for the front". Now, Liu Bocheng Factory headquarters, production workshops and other buildings are basically well preserved.

刘伯承工厂是全国唯一以共和国元帅名字命名的兵工厂，是人民兵工的优秀典范和杰出代表。"一切为了前线"的刘伯承工厂精神，是人民兵工精神的传承和弘扬，是人民兵工的宝贵精神财富。

Liu Bocheng Factory is the only munitions factory named after the Marshal of the People's Republic of China, and is an excellent example of the people's armory. The factory spirit of "all for the front" is the inheritance and promotion of the people's armed forces spirit, and is the precious spiritual wealth of the people's armed forces.

水塔。
Water tower.

山西

贰：核心物项
Section two: Core items

厂部，火工部工房，机工部工房，窑洞（双孔），总装部工房，火工库残墙，水塔，烟囱，朱德、彭德怀签发的任命书，生产计划等历史档案。

The factory buildings, the fire warehouse workshop, the machinery department workshop, the cave (double hole), the general assembly department workshop, fire warehouse remnant wall, water tower, chimney, appointment letter issued by Zhu De and Peng Dehuai, production plan and other historical archives.

火工库残墙。
Fire warehouse remnant wall.

遗产名称/位置:"刘伯承工厂"旧址/山西省长治市
Heritage name/Location: Former Site of Liu Bocheng Factory/Changzhi City, Shanxi Province

山西

总装部工房。
The general assembly department workshop.

总装部工房内景。
The general assembly department workshop.

27

叁：遗产活化
Section three: Revitalization

　　近年来，山西省长治市潞州区区委、区政府规划着手修复"刘伯承工厂"旧址，将其打造成集军工历史、革命传统教育、红色旅游观光、党的廉政教育于一体的红色文化品牌，形成独具特色的军工历史文化纪念馆。

　　In recent years, Changzhi Luzhou District Committee and Government of Shanxi Province have planned to restore the former site of "Liu Bocheng Factory" to build it into a red cultural brand integrating military industry history, revolutionary traditional education, red tourism and anti-corruption education of the CPC, and form a unique military history and culture Memorial Hall.

在刘伯承工厂厂部旧址上建设的山西省第五专署历史纪念馆，是山西省唯一一个保存完好的专员公署旧址，与刘伯承兵工厂共同构成长治市大型爱国主义教育基地。

The Fifth Historical Memorial Hall of Shanxi Province, built on the former site of Liu Bocheng Factory, is the only well preserved site of prefectural commissioner's office in Shanxi Province. It forms a large-scale patriotism education base in Changzhi City together with Liu Bocheng Factory.

遗产名称/位置：“刘伯承工厂"旧址/山西省长治市
Heritage name/Location: Former Site of Liu Bocheng Factory/Changzhi City, Shanxi Province

山西

机工部内景。
Interior of Mechanical Department.

石圪节煤矿

解放区的第一座红色煤矿
The First Red Coal Mine in the Liberated Area

壹：遗产春秋
Section one: History

位于山西省长治市的石圪节煤矿，成立于1926年，原名为裕丰公司（振华煤矿）。1945年8月18日，石圪节矿工配合八路军地方武装解放了矿山，成为中国共产党在解放区接收管理的第一座红色煤矿。

Found in 1962, Shigejie Coal Mine, formerly known as Yufeng Company (Zhenhua Coal Mine), was located in Changzhi City, Shanxi Province. On August 18th, 1945, Shigejie miners cooperated with local armed forces of the Eighth Route Army to liberate the mine. It became the first red coal mine that the CPC took over and managed in the liberated area.

遗产名称 / 位置：石圪节煤矿 / 山西省长治市
Heritage item/Location: Shigejie Coal Mine/Changzhi City Shanxi Province

阅读链接 Link for further reading

石圪节矿风
The spirit of Shigejie Coal Mine

1963年，石圪节煤矿被周恩来总理亲手树为全国工交战线勤俭办企业五面红旗之一，形成了"艰苦奋斗、勤俭办矿"的石圪节矿风。1991年，石圪节矿风报告团受到了江泽民等党和国家领导人的亲切接见。1995年，煤炭部设立"石圪节精神奖"。石圪节精神在煤炭战线不断发扬光大。

In 1963, with the spirit of "hardworking and thrifty", Shigejie Coal Mine was personally set up by Premier Zhou Enlai as one of the five red banners of running enterprises thriftily. In 1991, the Shigejie delegation was cordially received by Jiang Zemin and other leaders of CPC and China. In 1995, Ministry of Coal established "Shigejie Spirit Award" and thereafter the spirit was constantly being carried forward.

洗煤厂。
Coal preparation plant.

山西

20世纪80年代，石圪节煤矿用半套综采设备建成了全国首批现代化样板矿。2016年10月，根据国家煤炭行业供给侧结构性改革需要，石圪节煤矿成为山西省第一座完成去产能矿井关闭的煤矿。

In the 1980s, Shigejie Coal Mine made the first group of modern sample mine in China with half set of comprehensive mining equipment. In October 2016, it became the first coal mine in Shanxi Province to be closed, because of the needs of the supply-side structural reform in coal industry.

近百年来，石圪节煤矿先后荣获300多项省部级以上荣誉，涌现出许传珩、郝晓明、董爱花等一大批先进人物。其近百年的发展历程，浓缩了中国共产党领导下中国煤炭工业成长的轨迹，被称为中国煤矿的"西柏坡"。

In the past 100 years, Shigejie Coal Mine has won more than 300 provincial and ministerial honors, and a large number of advanced figures such as Xu Chuanheng, Hao Xiaoming and Dong Aihua. Shigejie Coal Mine has been called the "Xibaipo" of China's coal mines because of its nearly 100 years' development representing the growth track of China's coal industry under the leadership of the CPC.

贰：核心物项
Section two: Core items

　　南副立井、北副立井、主斜井；"三天轮"提升装置、洗煤厂及附属设施、更新厂 2 栋、职工集体宿舍 3 栋；苏式矿工俱乐部、1978 年建成的矿工俱乐部、裕丰煤矿工人抗日救国会旧址、康克清到石圪节煤矿传播革命火种旧址；清末生产的道轨、朝鲜机床；部分媒体报道、老照片、全国科学大会奖状等历史档案。

South auxiliary shaft, north auxiliary shaft, main inclined shaft, "three day wheel" lifting device, coal washing plant and its facilities, 2 renewal plants, 3 dormitory buildings, Soviet style miners club, miners' club built in 1978, former site of Yufeng coal workers' anti Japanese National Salvation Association, and the former site for spreading revolutionary fire from Kang Keqing to Shigejie Coal Mine, tracks produced in late Qing Dynasty, North Korean machine tools; some media newspapers, old photos, National Science Conference Awards and other historical archives.

老照片。
Old photos.

遗产名称/位置：石圪节煤矿/山西省长治市
Heritage item/Location: Shigejie Coal Mine/Changzhi City Shanxi Province

山西

南副立井。
South auxiliary shaft.

叁：遗产活化
Section three: Revitalization

自去产能关闭以来，石圪节煤矿以打造矿山机械设备露天博物园、国家矿山遗址公园、创建红色旅游示范基地等为抓手，探索去产能关闭老矿发展新路，在新时代赋予石圪节精神新内涵。

Since its closure, Shigejie Coal Mine has explored a new development route by means of building an open-air museum of mining machinery and equipment, building a national mine heritage park, and establishing red tourism demonstration base. In the new era, the spirit of Shigejie has been endowed with new connotation.

石艺节八一八文化广场（秦鸿彬摄）。
Shige Festival, bayi8 culture square (Photo by Qin Hongbin).

高平丝织印染厂

太行山上一枝花
A Flower on Taihang Mountain

壹：遗产春秋
Section one: History

  高平丝织印染厂始建于1958年，是我国"二五"计划重点项目。改革开放以后，高平丝织印染厂成为华北地区最大的丝绸国营企业，产品畅销国内各大、中城市，并远销美国、日本等地，被誉为"太行山上一枝花"。20世纪90年代在高平丝织印染厂基础上重组成立的晋城市凤凰织品有限公司，是山西潞绸的唯一传承单位。

  Gaoping Silk Printing and Dyeing Factory was found in 1958, which was the key project of the Second Five-year Plan in China. After the reform and opening up, Gaoping Silk Printing and Dyeing Factory had become the largest state-owned silk enterprise in North China and was known as "A flower on Taihang Mountain". Its products were sold well in large and medium-sized cities in China and exported to the United States and Japan.Established on the basis of Gaoping Silk Printing and Dyeing Factory in the 1990s, Jincheng Fenghuang Textile Co., Ltd. was the only inheriting unit of Shanxi Lu Silk.

1962年生产中使用的卷纬机。
A weft winding machine used in 1962.

1967年生产中使用的定型机和拉幅机。
Asetting machine and a tensioning machine used in 1967.

遗产名称/位置：高平丝织印染厂/山西省晋城市
Heritage item/Location: Gaoping Silk Printing and Dyeing Factory/Jincheng City Shanxi Province

阅读链接 Link for further reading

潞绸
Lu Silk

潞绸产于山西晋东南地区，因潞州而得名，始于隋，兴于唐，盛于明清，是山西丝绸业鼎盛时期的代表，历史上曾与杭锻、蜀锦齐名，名列中国三大名绸之一。

Produced in Southest region, Shanxi Province, Lu Silk was the representative of Shanxi silk industry. It was named after Luzhou (a district of Changzhi City). It began in the Sui Dynasty, rose in the Tang Dynasty, and flourished in the Ming and Qing Dynasties. Lu Silk, together with Hang Silk and Shu Brocade, was one of the three famous silk fabrics in China.

潞绸织造技艺全由手工完成，2014年入选国家级非物质文化遗产。织造工艺包括原料选用、经丝、纬丝、织机装造、纹制设计、纸板制作、织造和成品制作八个步骤。织造所用传统设备有手工轮经车、手工打纬车、络丝车、扶摇机、捻丝车、手工丝织机。产品包括真丝织锦被面、手帕、水纱、皱纱、提花绸、花软缎等。传统潞绸手感厚实、结实耐用。

In 2014, Lu Silk weaving skills, all completed by hand, was selected as A National Intangible Cultural Heritage. The weaving techniques involve the following eight steps: selection of raw material, warp yarn, weft yarn, loom assembly, pattern design, making paperboard, weaving and finished product manufacture. The traditional weaving equipment includes manual warp wheel, manual weft beating machine, winding machine, whirling machine, twisting machine and manual silk weaving machine. Pure silk brocade quilt cover, handkerchief, water yarn, crepe yarn, jacquard silk and soft satin are its products. The traditional Lu Silk feels thick and durable.

山西

1968年生产中使用的染丝机和绳状染色机。
Silk dyeing machines and rope dyeing machines used in 1968.

1963年生产中使用的浆丝机。
A pulp silk machine used in 1963.

贰：核心物项
Section two: Core items

  锯齿型联排厂房；卷纬机 3 台，浆丝机 1 台，定型机、拉幅机各 1 台，染丝机 2 台，绳状染色机 10 台，潞绸织造技艺。

  Zigzag row plants, 3 weft winding machines, 1 pulp silk machine, 1 setting machine, 1 tensioning machine, 2 silk dyeing machines, 10 rope dyeing machines; Lu Silk weaving technique.

织布机。
Loom.

络丝机。
Silk machine.

遗产名称/位置：高平丝织印染厂/山西省晋城市
Heritage item/Location: Gaoping Silk Printing and Dyeing Factory/Jincheng City Shanxi Province

叁：遗产活化
Section three: Revitalization

20世纪90年代以来，高平丝织印染厂经过数次改制，发展成为今天的山西吉利尔潞绸集团。公司在原高平丝织印染厂的基础上兴建和改造的潞绸文化园，是融合展示潞绸文化与品牌发展的文化产业创意园，拥有潞绸文化历史馆、手工工艺展示区、潞绸大学等功能区，将工业文化传承与创意设计、生产和教育等有机结合在一起。

Since the 1990s, Gaoping Silk Printing and Dyeing Factory has undergone several restructuring and developed into Shanxi Jilier Lu Silk Group. Built and renovated on the basis of the original Gaoping Silk Printing and Dyeing Factory, Lu Silk Cultural Park is a creative cultural industrial park and displays the culture and brand of Lu Silk. This cultural and creative industry park has some functional areas such as a Lu Silk Cultural and Historical Museum, a handicraft exhibition, and a Lu silk University, combining the inheritance of industrial culture with creative design, production and education.

吉利尔潞绸产品体验馆。
Jilier Lu Silk Product Experience Hall.

山西

国家工业遗产（第三批）

抚顺西露天矿

开采史最长的国有大型露天煤矿
A State-owned Open-pit Coal Mine with the Longest Mining Time

壹：遗产春秋
Section one: History

抚顺西露天矿位于抚顺煤田西部、浑河南岸、千台山北麓，开采于1901年，1914年转为露天开采，是国内露天开采史最长的国有大型露天煤矿。新中国成立以来，抚顺西露天矿累计产煤2.8亿吨、油母页岩5.3亿吨，为国家经济发展和建设做出了重大贡献。

Located in the West of Fushun coalfield, the South bank of Hun River and the North foot of Qiantai Mountain, West Open-pit Mine was the state-owned open-pit coal mine with the longest mining time in China. It was started in 1901 and switched to open-pit mining in 1914. Since the founding of the People's Republic of China, West Open-pit Mine had produced a total of 280 million tons of coal and 530 million tons of oil shale, making a significant contribution to the national economic development and construction.

遗产名称/位置：抚顺西露天矿 / 辽宁省抚顺市
Heritage item/Location: West Open-pit Mine/Fushun City Liaoning Province

辽宁

抚顺西露天矿矿坑全貌。
Full view of West Open-pit Mine.

贰：核心物项
Section two: Core items

矿坑，大型挖掘机 2 台、电力机车 4 辆、推土犁 1 台、108 吨采矿汽车 1 辆、蒸汽机车 2 辆。
Mine pit, 2 large excavators, 4 electric locomotives, a bulldozer plough, a 108-ton mining car, 2 steam locomotives.

蒸汽机车。A steam locomotive.

遗产名称/位置：抚顺西露天矿/辽宁省抚顺市
Heritage item/Location: West Open-pit Mine/Fushun City Liaoning Province

叁：遗产活化
Section three: Revitalization

　　抚顺西露天矿矿坑面貌壮观，技术保存完整，目前已全面实施矿坑生态恢复综合治理工作。在原址上兴建6 000多平方米的抚顺煤矿博物馆，以真切、翔实的编撰方略和展陈体例对抚顺煤矿的历史加以梳理呈现。党员教育基地更直观、艺术地展现了百年矿山的发展。文化长廊、红色记忆和百年露天小火车等板块，弘扬了百年企业文化、红色文化等特色文化。

　　West Open-pit Mine has a spectacular appearance and a complete technical preservation. At present, comprehensive work of mine ecological restoration has been carried out. It is planned to build the Fushun Coal Mine Museum of more than 6 000 square meters on the original site, which will present the history of Fushun coal mine with accurate compilation strategy and detailed exhibitions. The party member education base actively shows the development of mine in the past century. The Cultural Corridor, the Red Memory, the Hundred-year Open-air Train and other sections carry forward the century-old enterprise culture and the red culture.

抚顺西露天矿大型设备陈列广场。
Large-scale Equipment Exhibition Square of West open-pit Mine.

国家工业遗产（第三批）

营口造纸厂

共和国第一张凸版印刷纸的诞生地
The Birthplace of the First Relief Printing Paper in the People's Republic of China

壹：遗产春秋
Section one: History

营口造纸厂始建于1936年，由日本钟渊纺绩株式会社设立分支机构康德苇巴尔布股份有限公司筹建，当时名为康德苇巴尔布股份有限公司营口工厂，1946年被国民党资源委员会接收，改名为资源委员会辽宁纸浆造纸有限公司营口造纸厂，主要生产光纸。

Founded in 1936, Yingkou Paper Mill, then called Conde Wei-Barb Co., Ltd. Yingkou Plant, was built by Zhongyuan Textile Company Conde Wei-Barb Co., Ltd. In 1946, it was took over by Resources Commission of National Party and was renamed Liaoning Pulp and Paper Co., Ltd. Yingkou Paper Mill of Resources Commission. Glossy papesr were its main products.

新中国成立以后，营口造纸厂很快完成了生产恢复工作。1952年，总浆产量达到6万吨，成为当时全国最大的商品纸浆厂。1967年，营口造纸厂生产出了中国第一张凸版印刷纸，解决了印刷纸只能进口的问题，成为当时《毛泽东选集》的专用印刷纸。

After the founding of the People's Republic of China, Yingkou Paper Mill quickly completed the resumption of production. In 1952, Yingkou Paper Mill became the largest pulp mill in China, with a total pulp output of 60 000 tons. In 1967, Yingkou Paper Mill produced China's first relief paper, which solved the problem that printing paper could only be imported, and the relief paper became the special printing paper for *Selected Works of Mao Zedong*.

在60余载发展过程中，营口造纸厂完成了许多造纸机械和工艺技术的重大创新，创造了多个行业第一，同时，培养和向外输送了大批工程技术人员和管理人才，见证了我国造纸工业发展的历史进程，具有重要的历史价值、科技价值、社会价值和艺术价值。

In the course of more than 60 years of development, Yingkou Paper Mill had completed many major innovations in papermaking machinery and technology, and leaded many fields of the industry. At the same time, it had trained and sent a large number of engineering and technical personnel and management personnel. It witnessed the development of papermaking industry in China, which had important historical value, scientific value, social value and artistic value.

遗产名称 / 位置：营口造纸厂 / 辽宁省营口市
Heritage item/Location: Yingkou Paper Mill/Fushun City Liaoning Province

贰：核心物项
Section two: Core items

大罐厂房、切苇厂房、九号机厂房、十五号机厂房、157立方米的立式蒸煮锅3台、220立方米蒸煮锅4台、圆盘式切苇刀、干法除尘系统、3150长网多缸凸版纸机2台。

Large tank workshop, reed cutting workshop, No.9 workshop, No.15 workshop, 3 vertical cooking pots of 157 cubic meters, 4 cooking pots of 220 cubic meters, disk reed-cutting knife, dry dust removal system, 2 3150-long net multi-cylinder relief paper machines.

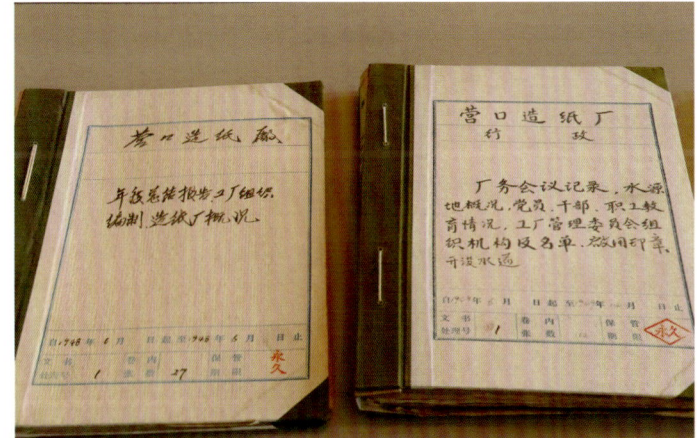

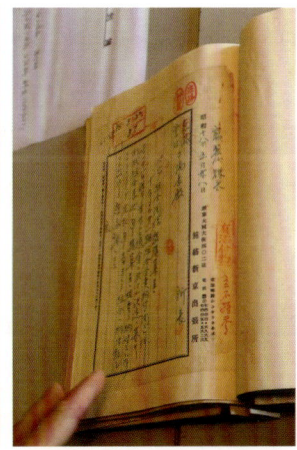

历史文献。
Historical Documents.

辽宁

国家工业遗产（第三批）

切苇厂房始建于1936年，1938年投产，南北长35米，东西宽64米，高20米，主要工序内容是将芦苇切成合格原料并筛去杂质。

The reed cutting workshop was built in 1936 and put into production in 1938. It was 35 meters long from North to South, 64 meters wide from East to West, and 20 meters high. The main process was to cut reeds into qualified raw materials and screen out impurities.

遗产名称/位置：营口造纸厂/辽宁省营口市
Heritage item/Location: Yingkou Paper Mill/Fushun City Liaoning Province

辽宁

3150长网多缸凸版纸机，经过三次大的技术改造，纸张年产量可达1.8万吨。
After three major technical modifications, the 3150 long net multi-cylinder relief paper machines can produce 18 000 tons of paper annually.

叁：遗产今夕
Section three: Current Situation

2010年7月，营口造纸厂停产。目前，工业遗产项目核心物项均保存完整，厂房和设备均留有人员看护。

In July 2010, Yingkou Paper Mill stopped production. At present, the core items of the industrial heritage project are well preserved. Its factory and equipments are under care.

厂区外景。
Exterior of the factory.

遗产名称 / 位置：营口造纸厂 / 辽宁省营口市
Heritage item/Location: Yingkou Paper Mill/Fushun City Liaoning Province

辽宁

大罐厂房始建于1936年，1938年投产，占地2 200平方米，为酸法造纸的核心车间，主要设备包括3台157立方米的立式蒸煮锅和4台220立方米的蒸煮锅及配套系统，规模为国内最大。
The large tank workshop was built in 1936 and put into production in 1938. It covered an area of 2 200 square meters and was the core workshop of acid paper making. The main equipment included three vertical cooking pots of 157 cubic meters, four cooking pots of 220 cubic meters and corresponding supporting systems, the scale of which was the largest in China.

大连冷冻机厂铸造工厂

东北制冷行业发展的缩影
The Epitome of the Development of Refrigeration Industry in Northeast China

壹：遗产春秋
Section one: History

　　大连冷冻机厂始建于1930年，前身是新民铁工厂，是辽宁省最早生产制冷设备的工厂。新中国成立后，新民铁工厂与国家合营成立大连冷冻机厂，是中国研制、生产各种类型制冷设备的大型骨干企业和出口成套制冷设备的主要企业，是全国制冷行业最先进的制冷产品性能测试基地，也是全国制冷行业唯一获得金质奖的企业。

　　Dalian Refrigeration Plant was founded in 1930, formerly known as Xinmin Iron Works, is the earliest refrigeration plant in Liaoning Province. After the founding of the People's Republic of China, Xinmin Iron Works and the State jointly established Dalian Refrigeration Plant, which was a major enterprise in China to develop and produce various types of refrigeration equipments and export complete sets of refrigeration equipments. It was the most advanced performance testing base of refrigeration products and the only enterprise that had won the gold award in the national refrigeration industry.

图为产业园内富有时代印记的生产设备。
The picture shows the production equipment with the era mark in the industrial park.

遗产名称/位置：大连冷冻机厂铸造工厂/辽宁省大连市
Heritage item/Location: Dalian Refrigerator Foundry/Dalian City Liaoning Province

大连冷冻机厂铸造工厂始建于20世纪50年代，是中华人民共和国成立之后，东北地区制冷工业萌芽、发展、改革、开放的缩影，以其不可再生性和独特性，成为记录中国制冷行业从制造业1.0不断升级、冷热产业链不断延伸发展历程的"活化石"，同时也是大连工业文明发展的重要组成部分。

Dalian Refrigerator Foundry, built in the 1950s, was the epitome of the born, development, reform and opening up of refrigeration industry in Northeast China after the founding of Peole's Republic of China. It was a "living fossil" with its non-renewable and uniqueness that recorded the upgrading of China's refrigeration industry from manufacturing 1.0, and the development of the cooling and heating industry chain. It is also an important part of the development of Dalian's industrial civilization.

辽宁

20世纪70年代铸造车间外景。
Exterior of the foundry in the 1970s.

贰：核心物项
Section two: Core items

铸造工厂厂房、迪砂3030机器设备、模具、历史档案及文献资料。
Workshops, DISA 3030 equipment, molds, historical documents.

20世纪90年代引进的迪砂生产线。
DISA production line introduced in the 1990s.

铸造工厂厂房外景。
Exterior of workshops of Dalian Refrigerator Foundry.

遗产名称/位置：大连冷冻机厂铸造工厂/辽宁省大连市
Heritage item/Location: Dalian Refrigerator Foundry/Dalian City Liaoning Province

叁：遗产活化
Section three: Revitalization

  1993年，大连冷冻机厂上市，如今已发展成为大连冰山集团有限公司。2017年，大连冰山集团有限公司整体搬迁。为了更好地开发和利用工业遗产，大连冰山集团有限公司对老厂区做了重新规划，运用全新的思维方式和理念，建设了面向未来的冰山慧谷智慧创新产业园，吸引了洛可可、盛世利、松下、富士、新华网等百余家知名企业品牌入驻。

  Dalian Refrigeration Plant was listed in 1993. Now it has developed into Dalian Bingshan Group Co., Ltd. In 2017, the whole Dalian Bingshan Group Co., Ltd. was relocated. In order to better develop the industrial heritage, Dalian Bingshan Group Co., Ltd. replanned the old site and build the Iceberg Wisdom Innovation Industrial Park through new ways of thinking. It has attracted more than 100 well-known enterprise brands, such as Rococo, Shengshili, Panasonic, Fuji and Xinhuanet.

辽宁

冰山慧谷智慧创新产业园内场景。
Scene of the Iceberg Wisdom Innovation Industrial Park.

国家工业遗产（第三批）

一重富拉尔基厂区

中国制造业的第一重地
The Most Important Place in China's Manufacturing Industry

壹：遗产春秋
Section one: History

　　作为涉及国家安全和国民经济命脉的骨干装备企业之一，中国一重建立于新中国百废待兴之时，始终秉承发展壮大民族装备工业的国家使命，为矿山、能源、钢铁、有色、化工、交通运输等行业及国防军工提供重大成套技术装备，周恩来总理誉之为"国宝"，习近平总书记赞誉其为"中国制造业的第一重地"。

　　As one of the backbone equipment enterprises involved in national security and the lifeblood of national economy, China First Heavy Industries was founded when all the waste was waiting to be revitalized. It has always been adhering to the national mission of developing national equipment industry, providing major complete sets of technical equipments for mining, energy, steel, nonferrous metal, chemical industry, transportation and national defense. Premier Zhou Enlai praised it as a "national treasure" and General Secretary Xi Jinping praised it as "the most important place in China's manufacturing industry".

中国一重坐落于黑龙江省齐齐哈尔市，前身为富拉尔基第一重型机器厂，始建于1954年，1959年主体厂房全部落成竣工，是"一五"计划期间建设的156项重点工程项目之一。为推动中国工业从无到有、由弱到强，实现工业独立自主、建设完备的工业体系和工业强国做出了艰辛努力和卓越贡献。

Located in Qiqihar City, Heilongjiang Province, the fomer of China First Heavy Industries is Fulaerji No. 1 Heavy Machinery Factory. The construction of China First Heavy Industries was started in 1954 and its main plant was completed in 1959. It is one of 156 key engineering projects constructed during the "First Five-year Plan" period. China First Heavy Industrieshas made remarkable contributions to promoting the development of China's industry.

遗产名称 / 位置：一重富拉尔基厂区 / 黑龙江省齐齐哈尔市
Heritage item/Location: China First Heavy Industries Fulaerji Plant Area/ Qiqihaer City, Heilongjiang Province

贰：核心物项
Section two: Core items

厂前广场毛泽东主席不锈钢塑像。
A stainless steel statue of Chairman Mao Zedong in front of the factory.

　　重型装备制造厂、热处理制造厂、水压机锻造厂、金属结构制造厂；12 500 吨自由锻造水压机、捷克产 6 000 吨水压机、苏联产 9 米立车、H3TC 车床、井式热处理炉沉箱等机器设备；建厂初期吊具等生产工具；开工纪念章、厂前广场毛泽东主席不锈钢塑像；历史档案。

Heavy equipment factory, heat treatment plant, hydraulic forging plant, metal structure manufacturing plant, 12 500 ton free forging hydraulic press, 6 000 ton hydraulic press made in Czech Republic, 9 m vertical car made in the Soviet union, H3TC lathe, caisson of well type heat treatment furnace and other equipments, lifting tools and other producing tools in the early stage of plant construction, commemorative medal for commencement of construction, a stainless steel statue of Chairman Mao Zedong in front of the factory, historical archives.

黑龙江

国家工业遗产
（第三批）

1 150 毫米初轧机全景。
Overall view of 1 150 mm blooming mill.

12 500 吨自由锻造水压机。
12 500 ton free forging hydraulic press.

1591立式车床由苏联于1959年生产，加工重量最大达250吨，最大工件直径13米，加工垂直精度可达0。
Vertical lathe made by the Soviet Union in 1959. The maximum machining weight is 250 tons, the maximum workpiece diameter is 13 meters, the vertical machining accuracy is 0.

遗产名称 / 位置： 一重富拉尔基厂区 / 黑龙江省齐齐哈尔市
Heritage item/Location:China First Heavy Industries Fulaerji Plant Area/ Qiqihaer City, Heilongjiang Province

叁：遗产活化
Section three: Revitalization

中国一重厂房具有苏式建筑的典型特征。厂区以自行设计并整体浇注的毛泽东主席塑像为中心，左右呈对称分布，参照苏联乌拉尔重机厂设计模式，依据生产工艺工序依次由南到北排列。

All the workshops of China First Heavy Industries have the typical characteristics of Soviet-style architecture. Referring to the design mode of Ural Heavy Machinery Factory in Soviet Union, China First Heavy Industries takes the statue of Chairman Mao Zedong, which is self-designed and fully cast, as the center and the left, and right sides are distributed symmetrically. According to the production process, it is arranged from south to north.

一重富拉尔基厂区旧照与现状。
Old photos and current situation of Fulaerji plant area of Yizhong.

黑龙江

国家工业遗产
（第三批）

　　在 1959 年建厂初期建成的中国一重主要厂房中，95% 以上仍在使用。随着产能的不断提升，部分车间和设备陆续进行了加长扩建和改造，以满足新时代生产的需求。

　　More than 95% of the main workshops of China First Heavy Industries built in the early stage of the construction in 1959 are still in use. In order to meet the needs of production in the new era and improve production capacity, some workshops and equipments have been extended and transformed.

《第一重机厂志》。
Factory records of China First Heavy Industries.

热处理车间现况。
Current status of heat treatment workshop.

遗产名称 / 位置：一重富拉尔基厂区 / 黑龙江省齐齐哈尔市

Heritage item/Location:China First Heavy Industries Fulaerji Plant Area/ Qiqihaer City, Heilongjiang Province

目前，遗址项目已成为当地的特色人文景观。2018年12月3日，中国一重展览馆正式开馆，通过文字、图片、视频、新媒体、人机互动等形式，向公众普及工业知识的同时，真实、生动、全面地再现了中国一重作为中国工业"母机"企业一次次冲破技术封锁、自主创新的奋斗足迹。

At present, the site has become a cultural landscape with local characteristics. On December 3rd, 2018, China First Heavy Industries Exhibition Hall officially opened. It popularizes industrial knowledge to the public through text, pictures, videos, new media and human-computer interaction. At the same time, it truly, vividly and comprehensively reproduces the company's struggle footprint of breaking through technical blockade and independent innovation as China's industrial "mother machine" enterprise.

黑龙江

金属结构制造厂现况。
Current status of Metal Structure Factory.

国家工业遗产（第三批）

龙江森工桦南森林铁路

森林工业的"活化石"
"Living Fossil" of Forest Industry

壹：遗产春秋
Section one: History

龙江森工桦南森林铁路始建于1952年，全长361.3千米，贯穿黑龙江省佳木斯市桦南县、七台河市勃利县和双鸭山市宝清县等地。在黑龙江省森工林区发展的历史上，被称作老"功臣"的森林窄轨小火车，曾为生产采伐忙碌不止，累计输送木材1 000多万立方米，有力支撑了国家建设。

Huanan Forest Railway of Longjiang Forest Industry was built in 1952, with a total length of 361.3 km. It runs through Huanan County in Jiamusi City, Boli County in Qitaihe City, and Baoqing County in Shuangyashan City, Heilongjiang Province.The busy forest narrow gauge train, known as "meritorious statesman", has transported more than 10 million cubic meters of wood, giving strong support to national construction.

20世纪八九十年代，国家实施天然林保护工程，加之森林资源锐减，木材产量不断下调直至停止采伐，小火车也逐步退出木材运输战线。之后，森林铁路主要用来运输红光地区开采的原煤，随着煤炭和矿产资源管理政策的调整，红光煤矿停止生产，森林铁路煤炭运输于2012年4月随之停止。至此，龙江森工桦南森林铁路结束了半个多世纪的运输历史。

In the 1980s and the 1990s, with the implementation of the natural forest protection project and the sharp decrease of forest resources, the timber production continued to decline until logging was stopped, the small train gradually stopped transporting wood. The railway is mainly used to transport raw coal mined in Hongguang area. After the adjustment of coal and mineral resources management policies, Hongguang coal mine stopped production, and the coal transportation was suspended in April 2012. Since then, Huanan Forest Railway of Longjiang Forest Industry has ended more than half a century of transportation history.

遗产名称 / 位置：龙江森工桦南森林铁路 / 黑龙江省佳木斯市
Heritage item/Location: Huanan Forest Railway of Longjiang Forest Industry / Jiamusi City, Heilongjiang Province

黑龙江

穿行在乡镇中的小火车。Small trains running through villages and towns.

国家工业遗产
（第三批）

穿行在林海雪原中的小火车。
A small train goes through the forest and snow.

遗产名称 / 位置：龙江森工桦南森林铁路 / 黑龙江省佳木斯市
Heritage item/Location: Huanan Forest Railway of Longjiang Forest Industry / Jiamusi City, Heilongjiang Province

贰：核心物项
Section two: Core items

　　6台28吨蒸汽机车及完整的森林铁路线、设备厂房和森林铁路运输的整套架构，包括森林铁路机加车间、外燃车间、内燃车间、烘炉车间、翻砂车间、车站及45千米窄轨铁路；120马力的内燃机车1台、240马力内燃机车1台、PB15型平板车50辆、YZ型54座客车车厢3辆、15吨棚车3辆、守车4辆、敞车4辆；森林铁路配套设施25处、配套设备40台，历史档案。

6 28-ton steam locomotives and a complete forest railway line, factory buildings and the whole framework of forest railway transportation including forest railway machining workshops, external combustion workshops, internal combustion workshops, oven workshop, foundry workshops, railway station and 45 kilometers narrow gauge railway, a 120 horsepower diesel locomotive, a 240 horsepower diesel locomotive, 50 PB15 flatcars, 3 YZ 54 seats railway carriages, 3 15-ton box wagons, four cabooses, 4 open wagons, 25 forest railway supporting facilities, 40 sets of supporting equipment, historical archives.

黑龙江

窄轨铁路。
Narrow gauge railway.

叁：遗产活化
Section three: Revitalization

　　如今，森工林区仅存的部分窄轨铁路成了森林工业的"活化石"，被国外蒸汽机研究会专家评为"世界范围内保存最完整的窄轨铁路"，被誉为"世界级旅游珍品"。

　　Today, the only part of the narrowgauge railway in forest industry area has become the "living fossil" of forest industry. It was appraised as "the most complete and well-preserved narrow gauge railway in the world" by the experts of Foreign Steam Engine Research Institute, and honored as "world-class tourism treasure".

龙江森工打造的旅游区夜景。
Night view of Longjiang forest industry.

遗产名称 / 位置：龙江森工桦南森林铁路 / 黑龙江省佳木斯市
Heritage item/Location: Huanan Forest Railway of Longjiang Forest Industry / Jiamusi City, Heilongjiang Province

　　2018 年，桦南林业局有限公司为培育壮大旅游业，让停运多年的小火车重新焕发生机。森林铁路旅游不仅传扬了龙江森工厚重的历史文化，更让游客了解了森林铁路的发展史，实现了对小火车的动态保护。在小火车运行的一年多时间内，森林铁路旅游项目已累计接待国内外游客 5 万多人次。

In 2018, in order to cultivate and expand the tourism industry, Huanan Forestry Bureau Co., Ltd. revived the small train which had been out of service for many years. Forest railway tourism not only carries forward the rich history and culture of Longjiang Forest Industry, but also makes tourists understand the history of forest railway, realizes the dynamic protection of the Small train. Through the forest railway tourism project, the small train has received more than 50 000 domestic and foreign tourists in the running time of more than one year.

黑龙江

森工林区保存的窄轨铁路和机车。
Narrow gauge railways and locomotives preserved in forest industrial areas.

国家工业遗产（第三批）

上海造币厂

上海造币厂开启现代铸币时代
Shanghai Mint Opens the Era of Modern Coinage

壹：遗产春秋
Section one: History

上海造币厂始建于 1920 年，于 1994 年被列为上海市优秀历史建筑，2007 年，"钱币生产的手工雕刻技艺"被列入上海市非物质文化遗产名录，2014 年被列为上海市文物保护单位。

Shanghai Mint was built in 1920 and was listed as Excellent Historical Building in Shanghai in 1994. In 2007, the Art of Carving Coins by Hand was listed in the Intangible Cultural Heritage of Shanghai. In 2014, it was rated as a Cultural Relics Preservation Unit in Shanghai.

民国二十一年"上三鸟"一元银币，1933 年铸造。
The 21-year of the Republic of China "three birds" on the one-yuan silver coin, minted in 1933.

2008 年上海造币厂顺利完成北京奥运会系列纪念币和"金镶玉"奖牌的生产任务。
In 2008, Shanghai Mint successfully completed the production tasks of Beijing Olympic Games series commemorative coins and "Gold and Jade" medals.

66

遗产名称/位置：上海造币厂/上海市
Heritage item/Location: Shanghai Mint/Shanghai City

20世纪30年代，上海造币厂使用的近代机器加工带来了造币业全新的工艺流程，合乎现代铸币工艺及造币工业的要求。曾铸造国币"船洋"，推动"废两改元、统一币制"的金融改革。中华人民共和国成立后，陆续生产了四套人民币流通硬币，为保障国民经济的正常运行而恪尽职守。新中国第一套纪念金币、第一套熊猫金币、第一套普通纪念币也都诞生于此，丰富完善了币种结构，开创了我国纪念币事业的新局面。具备悠久的历史底蕴和雄厚的综合实力的上海造币厂，开启现代铸币工艺及造币工业时代；建成我国首个也是唯一的、当时世界最大的钢芯镀镍坯饼生产线，开辟了人民币硬币材质的新时代；拥有全流程生产体系：图稿设计、模具制造、生产压印，到技术保障、装备配套、综合管理；参与研制的YBW150国产卧式压印机填补了国内行业领域技术空白，摆脱了长期以来依赖进口的局面；"钱币生产的手工雕刻技艺"被纳入上海市非物质文化遗产名录。2008年，该厂更名为上海造币有限公司。

In the 1930s, the modern machine processing used by Shanghai Mint brought new technological process to the coinage industry, meeting the requirements of modern coinage technology and coinage industry. It minted the national currency "ship ocean", and promoted the financial reform of "Switch to Silver Dollar and Unifying the Currency System". Since the founding of the People's Republic of China, four sets of RMB coins have been produced in succession ensuring the normal operation of the national economy. China's first set of Commemorative Gold Coins, the First Set of Panda Gold Coins, the first set of Ordinary Commemorative Coins were also born here, perfecting the structure of the currency and creating a new situation in China's commemorative coin industry. Shanghai Mint with rich history and strong strength opened the era of modern coinage technology and coinage industry. The production line for steel core nickel plating cake it established was the first in China and the largest in the world and thereafter ushered in a new era for coin-making metal. It has a whole process of production system: draft design, mold manufacturing, production and embossing, technical support, equipment supporting and comprehensive management.The domestic YBW150 horizontal printing machine, Shanghai Mint participated in its production, has filled the technological gap in the domestic industry and got rid of the dependence on imports for a long time. The Art of Carving Coins by Hand has been included in the Intangible Cultural Heritage List of Shanghai. In 2008, the factory changed its name to Shanghai Mint Co., Ltd..

21世纪上海造币厂厂区俯瞰图。
An aerial view of Shanghai Mint in 21st century.

上海

贰：核心物项
Section two: Core items

办公楼，国民政府期间财政部部库旧址，蓄水塔；万两天平，轧机，冲床，光边机，美式压印机，仿法雕刻机，翻模机。
Office building, the former site of the Treasury Department warehouse during the National Government, water storage tower; Wanliang Balance, rolling mill, punch, edge rimming machine, American minting press, French style engraving machine, die press machine

轧机。
Rolling mill.

美式压印机。
American minting press.

遗产名称/位置：上海造币厂/上海市
Heritage item/Location: Shanghai Mint/Shanghai City

上海

万两天平称重。
Weigh with Wanliang Balance.

熊猫金币图稿。
Draft designs of Panda Gold Coin.

钱币生产中的手工雕刻技艺，已被上海市人民政府列入非物质文化遗产。
The Art of Carving Coins by Hand has been included by the Intangible Cultural Heritage in Shanghai.

国家工业遗产（第三批）

20世纪30年代拍摄的办公楼及蓄水塔。
Office building and water storage tower in the 1930s.

蓄水塔现状。
Current status of water storage tower.

20世纪30年代拍摄的财政部部库旧址。
The former site of the Treasury Department warehouse in the 1930s.

财政部部库（现名银行仓库）现状。
Current status of Treasury Department warehouse (current name: bank warehouse).

遗产名称/位置：上海造币厂/上海市
Heritage item/Location: Shanghai Mint /Shanghai City

叁：遗产活化
Section three: Revitalization

上海造币厂办公大楼及博物馆现状外景。
Exterior view of Shanghai Mint office building and museum.

上海造币博物馆馆内场景。
A scene in Shanghai Coinage Museum.

　　自纳入国家及地方文化遗产保护体系后，上海造币厂从人才队伍建设、馆校合作、非遗传承等方面搭建行业学术平台，并在2005年建成上海造币博物馆。博物馆开馆以来，积极履行国民金融教育的社会责任，开展校企合作，设立现场教学点，同时依托国家级硬币设计开发中心，围绕自身资源跨界合作，开发系列文创产品，并通过组织企业文化开放日活动，邀请普通市民进入博物馆零距离体验货币文化。另外，上海造币厂积极探索工业旅游发展模式，实地考察世界主流造币厂及造币博物馆运营模式、上海工业旅游景点等，与上海市工业旅游促进中心达成合作，大力传播货币文化。

　　Since it was incorporated into the national and local cultural heritage protection system, Shanghai Mint has set up an academic platform for the industry from the aspects of talent team construction, museum-school cooperation and non-genetic inheritance, and established the Shanghai Coinage Museum in 2005. Since the opening of the museum, it has actively fulfilled the social responsibility of national financial education. Relying on the National Coin Design and Development Center and its own resources, it carries out school-enterprise cooperation, sets up on-site teaching points, and develops a series of cultural and creative products. Through the organization of corporate culture Open Day activities, ordinary citizens are invited to enter the museum to experience the currency culture. After investigating the operation mode of the world's mainstream mint and coinage museum and Shanghai's industrial tourist attractions, Shanghai Mint reaches a cooperation with Shanghai Industrial Tourism Promotion Center, vigorously spreading the currency industrial culture.

上海

国家工业遗产（第三批）

常州恒源畅厂

运河沿岸工业遗存保护的常州样本
A Changzhou Sample Along the Canal used to Protect the Industrial Heritage

壹：遗产春秋
Section one: History

　　20世纪30年代初，三个年轻人在江苏省常州市三堡街集资兴办三和布厂。1933年，润源色布店老板毛锡章接手了经营不善的三和布厂，改名恒源布厂。1936年，恒源畅染织股份有限公司成立。1966年，恒源畅染织厂转变为完全国营的常州第五棉织厂。1980年，考虑到产品的更新和丰富，常州第五棉织厂再度更名为常州第五毛纺织厂，成为能生产纯化纤、混纺和全羊毛毛毯的全能工厂。20世纪90年代末，随着国家产业结构调整，常州第五毛纺织厂也开始走下坡路，直至2007年完全停产。

　　In the early 1930s, three young people raised money to set up Sanhe Cloth Factory in Sanbao street, Changzhou City, Jiangsu Province. In 1933, Mao Xizhang, the owner of Run Yuan Se cloth shop, took over the poorly managed Sanhe cloth factory and renamed it Heng Yuan Cloth Factory. In 1936, Heng Yuan Chang Dyeing & Weaving Co., Ltd. was established. In 1966, Heng Yuan Chang Dyeing & Weaving Plant was transformed into a fully state-owned cotton textile mill, called Changzhou No.5 Cotton Mill. In 1980, Considering the updating and enrichment of products, Changzhou No.5 Cotton Mill changed its name to Changzhou No.5 Wool Textile Factory, which could produce pure chemical fiber, blend and all-wool blankets. In the late 1990s, because of the adjustment of China's industrial structure, Changzhou No.5 Wool Textile Factory began to decline until it was completely shut down in 2007.

恒源畅厂全景。
Panorama of Heng Yuan Chang Plant.

遗产名称/位置：常州恒源畅厂 / 江苏省常州市
Heritage item/Location: Changzhou Heng Yuan Chang Plant /Changzhou City, Jiangsu Province

2008年，结合古运河申遗、常州申报国家历史文化名城，围绕"运河文化、工业遗存、创意产业"三大主题，通过抢救、保护、利用的办法，常州产业投资集团有限公司将原第五毛纺织厂改造成运河边的创意街区，成为古运河上一道独特的风景。

In 2008, considering the application for world heritage of the ancient canal and the declaration of Changzhou as a national historical and cultural city, and focusing on the three themes of canal culture, industrial heritage and creative industry, Changzhou Industrial Investment Group Co., Ltd. transformed the Changzhou No.5 Wool Textile Factory into a creative block along the canal by means of rescue, protection and utilization, which had become a unique landscape on the ancient canal.

阅读链接 Link for further reading

"恒源畅"的由来
The origin of "Heng Yuan Chang"

1933年，润源色布店老板将三和布厂改名恒源布厂。"恒"寓意长久，"源"取自"润源色布店"，此后恒源布厂得以发展。1936年，恒源畅染织股份有限公司成立，原厂名后增加了代表兴旺发达、财源旺盛的"畅"字。

In 1933, the owner of Run Yuan Se Cloth Shop changed the name of Sanhe Cloth Factory to Heng Yuan Cloth Factory. "Heng" means eternity, and "Yuan" comes from "Run Yuan Se Cloth Shop". Henceforth, Heng Yuan Cloth Factory developed. In 1936, Heng Yuan Chang Dyeing & Weaving Co., Ltd. was established. The company added a word "Chang" after the name of the original factory, representing prosperity.

中华人民共和国成立后，更名为常州第五毛纺织厂的恒源畅，生产棉细布、靛蓝劳动卡、童鹰毛毯等产品红极一时的抢手面料和床上用品，远销国内外。其中，童鹰毛毯是改制后的第五毛纺织厂响当当的牌子。

After the founding of the People's Republic of China, Heng Yuan Chang Dyeing & Weaving Co., Ltd. was renamed as Changzhou No.5 Wool Textile Factory. It produced popular fabrics such as cotton muslin, Denim and Tongying blanket and bedclothes, which were sold at home and abroad. Among the products, Tongying blanket is the most famous brand of Changzhou No.5 Wool Textile Factory.

江苏

中华民国时期国民革命军陆军一级上将冯玉祥为恒源畅题写的厂名牌匾拓件。
The rubbing of the plaque of the factory's name inscribed by Feng Yuxiang who was the first class general of the national revolutionary army during the Republic of China.

贰：核心物项
Section two: Core items

纺织车间 2 栋，电工间，高配间，木工间，锅炉房，机修车间，清末砖木结构建筑，办公楼 5 栋，工人食堂，女工宿舍，医务室。

2 textile workshops, electricians' room, switchgear room, carpenters' room, boiler room, machine repair shop, brick and wood structure buildings in the late Qing Dynasty, 5 office buildings, workers' canteen, women's dormitories and infirmary.

梳毛机和水喷淋空调装置，印染轧机和定型设备，纡子车，石槽 2 个，恒源厂界碑，雷明顿英文打字机，双鸽牌中文打字机；清光绪二年土地买卖契约、冯玉祥题写厂名牌匾拓件、民国 36 年的产权证明单等历史档案。

Carding machine and water spraying air conditioner, printing and dyeing mill and shaping equipment, winding cart, 2 stone grooves, boundary marker of Heng Yuan Factory, Remington English typewriter, Double-dove Chinese typewriter; the land sale contract in the second year of Emperor Guangxu in Qing Dynasty, the rubbing of the plaque of the factory's name inscribed by Feng Yuxiang, the property rights certificate in the 36th year of the Republic of China and other historical files.

原址保留的水喷淋空调装置。
The original water spraying air conditioner.

20 世纪 20 年代纺织工业的特征设备纡子车。
Winding cart, representative equipment for the textile industry in the 1920s.

遗产名称 / 位置：常州恒源畅厂 / 江苏省常州市
Heritage item/Location: Changzhou Heng Yuan Chang Plant /Changzhou City, Jiangsu Province

1936年建造的原恒源畅办公楼。
The original office building of Heng Yuan Chang built in 1936.

恒源畅厂老厂门。
The original gate of Heng Yuan Chang Plant.

江苏

叁：遗产活化
Section three: Revitalization

五号码头。
Pier No.5.

由原机修车间改造的五号剧场。
Theater No.5 transformed from the original machine repair shop.

2008年，运河五号创意街区项目建设启动后，建厂初期的老办公楼变身恒源畅书坊，经编车间被改造为档案博览中心，设有"常州百年工商档案展示馆""常州市全国劳模档案展示馆""龙城记忆-常州档案史料陈列馆"三大主题展馆；机修车间成为五号剧场，原部分纺织车间和风机廊道被改造成为恒源畅陈列馆。

In 2008, the construction of Canal No.5 Creative Block project was launched. The old office building was transformed into Heng Yuan Chang Bookshop, the warp knitting workshop was turned into the archives exhibition center, with three theme pavilions: "Changzhou Centennial industrial and Commercial Archives Exhibition Hall", "Changzhou National Labor Model Archives Exhibition Hall" and "Longcheng Memory-Changzhou Archives and Historical Materials Exhibition Hall"; The machine repair shop became theater No.5, and part of the original textile workshop and fan gallery were transformed into Heng Yuan Chang Exhibition Hall.

经过多年发展，依托恒源畅厂旧址建立的运河五号创意街区，已成为常州人触摸历史、寻找乡愁的精神家园，年均接待国内外各类考察团队200多批次，参观人数累计达420万人次，成为国企保护工业遗产的示范性代表。

After many years of development, Canal No.5 Creative Block has become a spiritual home of Changzhou memories. It has received more than 200 investigation teams at home and abroad every year, with a total number of 4.2 million visitors. It has become a model representative of state-owned enterprises in protecting industrial heritage.

遗产名称/位置：常州恒源畅厂 / 江苏省常州市
Heritage item/Location: Changzhou Heng Yuan Chang Plant /Changzhou City, Jiangsu Province

写有"运河记忆"的水塔。
A water tower with "Canal Memory" written on it.

纺织厂的机器设备与烟囱交相辉映。
The machinery and equipment of the textile mill are in harmony with the chimneys.

江苏

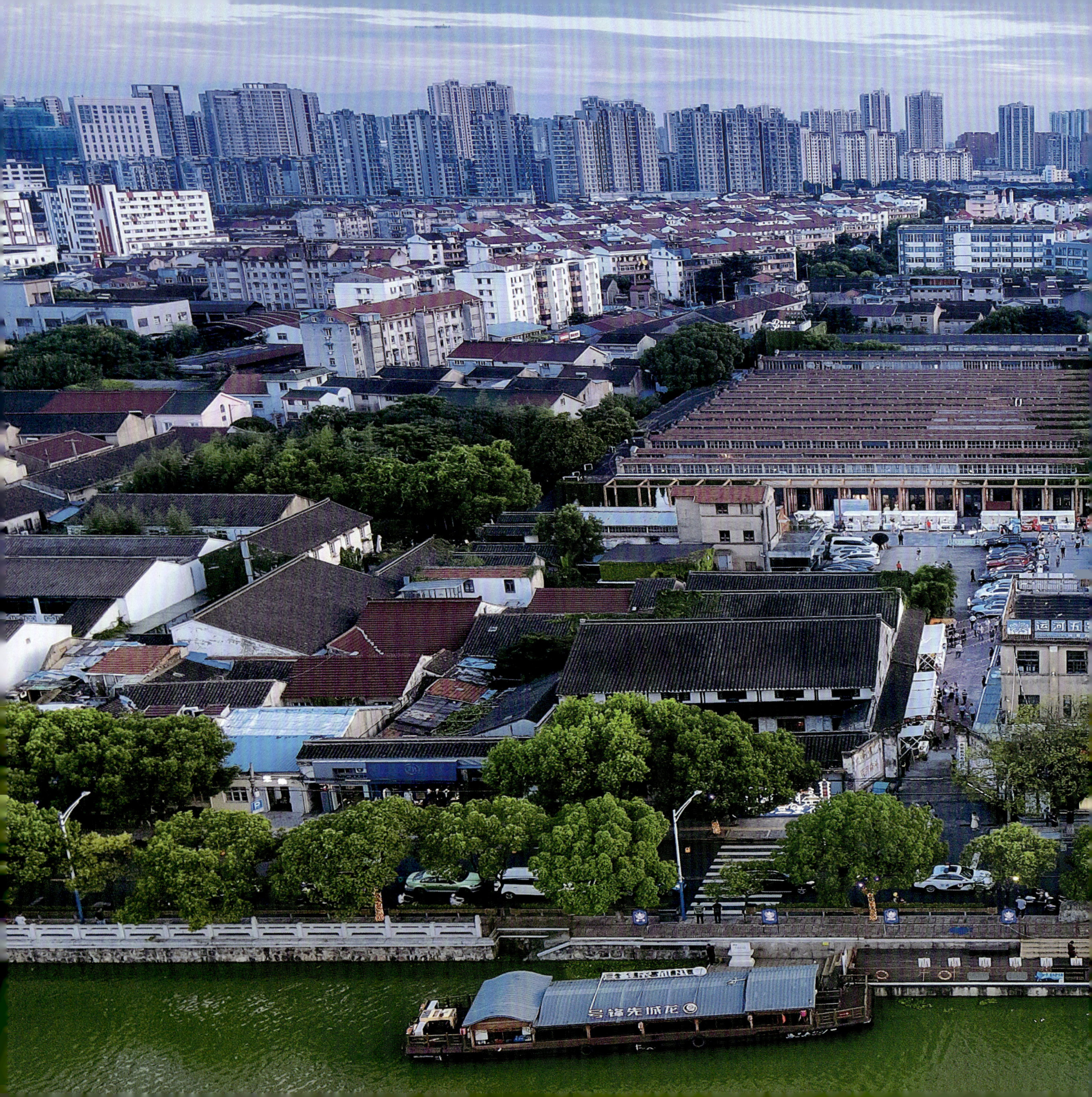
号锋先城龙
运河五

恒源畅厂区鸟瞰图,紧邻中国大运河常州城区段。
An aerial view of the Hengyuanchang factory area, adjacent to the Changzhou section of the Chinese Grand Canal.

国家工业遗产（第三批）

恒顺镇江香醋传统酿造区

食醋酿造业的"活化石"
A "Living Fossil" in Vinegar Brewing Industry

壹：遗产春秋
Section one: History

　　江苏恒顺醋业股份有限公司前身为"朱恒顺糟坊"，创建于1840年，历经百年变迁，集镇江传统制醋技艺之所长，以自家酒糟为主要原料，探索出独特的恒顺固态分层发酵技艺。如今，以恒顺香醋为代表的镇江香醋已成为中国"四大名醋"之一。

　　Jiangsu Hengshun Vinegar Co., Ltd., formerly known as "Zhu Hengshun Grocery Store", was founded in 1840. After a hundred years of development, the company has taken full advantage of Zhenjiang traditional vinegar brewing skills and with their own vinasse as the main raw material, it has been able to ferment from layered solid. Today, Hengshun Spiced Vinegar, representative of Zhenjiang Spiced Vinegar, has become one of the "Four Famous Vinegar" in China.

以恒顺老作坊为中心建设的中国醋文化博物馆全景。
Panorama of Chinese Vinegar Culture Museum around Hengshun old workshop.

遗产名称/位置： 恒顺镇江香醋传统酿造区 / 江苏省镇江市
Heritage item/Location: Hengshun Zhenjiang Spiced Vinegar Traditional Brewing Area/ Zhenjiang City, Jiangsu Province.

　　作为代表我国传统食醋生产工艺最高水平，以及为数不多仍"活着"的工业遗产，恒顺老作坊完整保留了具有千年历史的镇江香醋传统生产工艺，集物质文化遗存和非物质文化遗产为一体，是中国制醋发展史的实景呈现，具有重要的历史、科技、社会及艺术价值。

　　Hengshun old workshop, reflecting the highest level of China's traditional vinegar brewing process and being one of a small number of industrial heritages survived till now, completely retained Zhenjiang spiced vinegar traditional production process with thousands of years of history. It has both material-and-cultural relics and intangible cultural heritage, exhibiting the development of Chinese vinegar history. It is of important historical, scientific, social and artistic value.

贰：核心物项
Section two: Core items

　　传统晒醋场，恒顺荣炳老厂房，恒顺老作坊，传统酒窖，老门楼，恒顺米业老厂房；传统制醋工具，传统制酒工具；晚清时期营业执照，民国时期商标证书，建国初期的生产资料记录，20世纪六七十年代商标、印章；镇江恒顺香醋酿制技艺。

　　Traditional vinegar basking farm, Hengshun Rongbing old factory building, Hengshun old workshop, traditional wine cellar, old door building, Hengshun rice-industry old factory building, traditional vinegar-making tools, traditional wine-making tools, business license from late Qing Dynasty, trademark certificate of the Republic of China, record of production materials in the early period of the People's Republic of China, trademarks and seals in the 1960s and 1970s, Zhenjiang Hengshun Spiced Vinegar Brewing Skills.

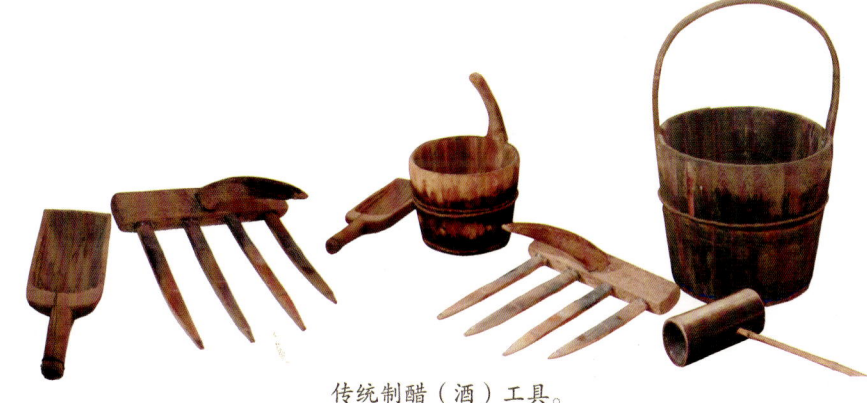

传统制醋（酒）工具。
Traditional vinegar-making / wine-making tools.

1931年恒顺的报纸广告。
Ads of Hengshun in newspaper in 1931.

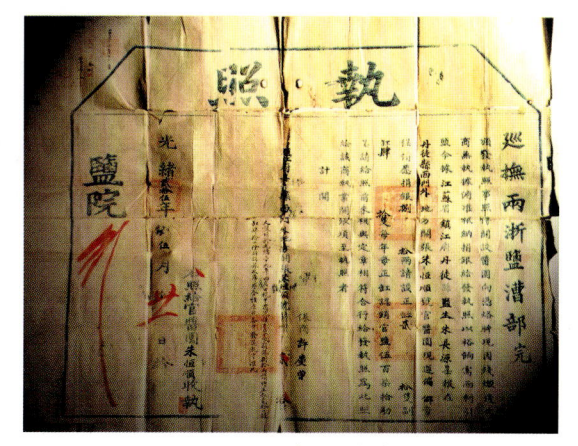

晚清时期恒顺营业执照。
Business license from late Qing Dynasty.

江苏

恒顺老作坊。
Hengshun old workshop.

遗产名称/位置：恒顺镇江香醋传统酿造区 / 江苏省镇江市
Heritage item/Location: Hengshun Zhenjiang Spiced Vinegar Traditional Brewing Area/ Zhenjiang City, Jiangsu Province.

恒顺米业老厂房。
Hengshun rice-industry old factory building.

传统晒醋场。
Traditional vinegar basking farm.

李友芳(1903—1981)，恒顺历史上的掌门人。作为一位爱国资本家，李友芳致力于民族工业发展，壮大恒顺香醋，支持公私合营改造，并将个人财产全部捐献给国家，受人敬仰。

Li Youfang (1903-1981) was a legendary figure in Hengshun history. As a patriotic capitalist, Li Youfang was committed to national industrial development, the expansion of Hengshun spiced vinegar and public-private joint venture transformation. She donated her personal property to the country and was well respected.

乔贵清，"镇江恒顺香醋酿制技艺"国家级非遗传承人。在传承古法酿造技艺的基础上，乔贵清不断推进技术工艺创新，为恒顺制醋技艺领跑中国醋业贡献了聪明才智。

Qiao Guiqing, successor of "Zhenjiang Hengshun Spiced Vinegar Brewing Skills"—National Intangible Cultural Heritage, inherited and passed on the ancient brewing skills. Qiao Guiqing pursued technological innovation successively and contributed his wisdom to Hengshun vinegar technology, making it the head of Chinese vinegar industry.

叁：遗产活化
Section three: Revitalization

20世纪90年代初，恒顺开始对车间、作坊、厂房、仓库等进行相应的保护、修缮和复原。目前，园区内还完整保存了20世纪五六十年代的车间、晒醋场，厂区内设施、设备基本保存了20世纪六七十年代的风貌。2008年，江苏恒顺醋业股份有限公司在"朱恒顺糟淋坊"的车间原址上修建老作坊，以老作坊为中心建立起中国醋文化博物馆，并以工业旅游的形式向社会开放，完整展现了恒顺制醋的工业形态和遗产文化。

In the early 1990s, Hengshun began to protect, repair and restore plants, workshops, factories, warehouses, etc. At present, workshops and vinegar basking farm in the 1950s and 1960s are fully preserved in the park. Facilities and equipments are preserved basically the style that of 1960s and 1970s. In 2008, Jiangsu Hengshun Vinegar Co., Ltd. built an old workshop on the original site of the workshop of "Zhuhengshun Grocery Store" and established the Chinese Vinegar Culture Museum. It was opened to the public in the form of industrial tourism, and showed to the public the industrial landscape and heritage culture of Hengshun Vinegar.

在朱恒顺精淋坊车间原址上修建的老作坊．
Old workshop built on the original site of the workshop of "Zhuhengshun Grocery Store".

国家工业遗产（第三批）

洋河老窖池群及酿酒作坊

中国白酒工业的典型遗产
A Typical Heritage of Chinese Liquor Industry

壹：遗产春秋
Section one: History

洋河老窖池群始建于明代，经历了明代、清代、民国、新中国四个时期，被誉为"中国白酒窖池活化石"，是国内保存最完整、数量最多、使用时间最长、微生物种类最丰富的酿酒窖池群之一。洋河老酿酒作坊始建于20世纪40年代，70余年不间断生产，见证了我国传统白酒产业的传承和发展。目前，洋河老窖池群及酿酒作坊的工业形态保存完整且仍在使用，是中国白酒工业的典型遗产。

Yanghe Old Pits Group was founded in the Ming Dynasty. Thereafter, it had experienced four periods: Ming Dynasty, Qing Dynasty, the Republic of China and the People's Republic of China. As the best-preserved and the most time-honored pits group with the most pits and the richest microbial species, it was crowned as the "Living Fossil of Chinese Liquor Pits". Since its establishment in the 1940s, Yanghe Wine-making workshops had been brewing wine continuously for more than 70 years, and had played a key role in the inheritance andprogress of China's traditional liquor industry.At present, Yanghe Old Pits group and wine-making workshops are well preserved and still in use, making them typical heritage of Chinese liquor industry.

酒厂建厂初期大门。
Original gate of the old wine-making factory.

遗产名称/位置：洋河老窖池群及酿酒作坊 / 江苏省宿迁市
Heritage item/Location: Yanghe Old Pits Group and Wine-making Workshops /Suqian City, Jiangsu Province

贰：核心物项
Section two: Core items

明清窖池，建国初期酿酒厂房，五十年代一号酒库，六十年代二号酒库，七十年代地下酒窖；清代和近代陶坛；历史档案；洋河酒传统酿造技艺。

Pits in Ming and Qing Dynasties, wine-making workshops in the early period of the People's Republic of China, No.1 wine storehouse in the 1950s, No.2 wine storehouse in the 1960s, wine cellar in the 1970s, pottery jars in Qing Dynasty and modern times, historical archives, traditional wine-making techniques of Yanghe.

建于20世纪60年代的二号酒库外景。
Exterior of No.2 wine storehouse in the 1960s.

清代和近代陶坛。
Pottery jars of Qing Dynasty and modern times.

20世纪50年代的洋河老酿酒作坊厂区。
Yanghe old wine-making work shops in the 1950s.

建国初期投入使用的酿酒厂房内景。
Interior of wine-making workshops put in use in the early period of the people's Republic of China.

江苏

国家工业遗产（第三批）

建于20世纪50年代的一号酒库外景。
Exterior of No.1 wine storehouse in the 1950s.

遗产名称 / 位置：洋河老窖池群及酿酒作坊 / 江苏省宿迁市
Heritage item/Location: Yanghe Old Pits Group and Wine-making Workshops /Suqian City, Jiangsu Province

建于20世纪70年代的地下酒窖入口。
Entrance of underground wine cellar in the 1970s.

叁：遗产活化
Section three: Revitalization

　　依托洋河老窖池群、地下酒窖等工业遗产，苏酒集团（洋河股份）在保证遗产不受破坏的前提下，建设了中国白酒活态博物馆群，进行洋河酒文化宣传，以馆群文化价值带动提升品牌价值。

　　In order to promote the culture of Yanghe Wine and thereafter to enhance its brand value, Sujiu Group (Yanghe Co., Ltd.) built a Chinese Liquor Ecomuseum Group out of the industrial heritages such as old pits group and underground cellars on the condition that those industrial heritages are not destroyed.

　　秉承严格保护、合理利用的理念，洋河老窖池群及酿酒作坊遗址项目打造了酿造体验、遗址展示、酒道表演、酒窖探秘、黄杨祈福、产品展示等一系列旅游产品，让公众感受江淮派浓香型白酒酿造文化的魅力。

　　Adhering to the concept of adequate protection and rational utilization, the project of Yanghe Old Pits Group and Wine-making workshops has created a series of tourism products, such as brewing experience, site display, liquor art performance, cellar exploration, Huangyang blessing and product display, so that the public can get the charm of the brewing culture of Jianghuai strong aromatic liquor.

手工酿酒作坊。
Craft wine-making workshops.

陶坛库内景。
Interior of pottery jars warehouse.

老窖池群。Old Pits Group.

国家工业遗产（第三批）

绍兴鉴湖黄酒作坊

汲取门前鉴湖水 "一冬一酿"黄酒香

Drawing Water from Jianhu Lake and Brewing One Type of Yellow Rice Wine Throughout Winter Time

壹：遗产春秋
Section one: History

绍兴鉴湖黄酒作坊，始创于清代雍正年间，由绍兴章氏家族在鉴湖源头创建而成。因毗邻鉴湖，开门见湖，取名"鉴湖"字号，凭借技艺精良，风味独特，闻名遐迩。至20世纪40年代，已是一家年产1 000缸的知名大酿坊。1982年后由绍兴市糖业烟酒公司管理，称鉴湖酿酒总厂。1997年酒厂被中国绍兴黄酒集团收购后，称中国绍兴黄酒集团鉴湖酿酒厂。2009年公司改制，更名为绍兴鉴湖酿酒有限公司。

Shaoxing Jianhu Yellow Rice Wine Workshop was founded by the Zhang family of Shaoxing at the source of Jianhu Lake during the reign of Emperor Yongzheng of Qing Dynasty. Because the workshop was around Jianhu lake, so it took the name of "Jianhu". It was well-known for its fine craftsmanship and unique flavor. Until the 1940s, it had grown into a famous brew house, brewing 1000 vats of wine every year. It was taken over by Shaoxing Sugar Tobacco and Liquor Company since 1982 and was renamed as Jianhu Head Liquor Factory. After merged by China Shaoxing Rice Wine Group in 1997, it turned into China Shaoxing Rice Wine Group Jianhu Brewery, and was renamed as Shaoxing Jianhu Brewery Co., Ltd. after its restructuring in 2009.

绍兴鉴湖黄酒作坊，占地5万平方米，目前仍保存着大量历史留存下来的清代、民国和新中国成立初期的老建筑。始终遵循"一冬一酿"的酿制古法，用独特的复式发酵工艺发酵90余天，翌年立春压榨、煎酒，然后泥封贮藏，一般贮存3年以上方可上市销售。鉴湖牌绍兴酒，是全国八大名酒之一，也是绍兴酒的第一个注册商标。绍兴鉴湖酿酒有限公司是首批获得绍兴酒原产地域产品保护的单位，中华老字号企业及"绍兴黄酒传统酿制工业遗产保护基地"。

Covering an area of 50 000 square meters, Shaoxing Jianhu Yellow Wine Workshop still retains a large number of historic buildings from Qing Dynasty, the Republic of China and the early period of the People's Republic of China. Following the ancient brewing method of "brewing yellow rice wine throughout winter time", Shaoxing Yellow Rice Wine was made through a unique compound fermentation process, featured by the fermentation of over 90 days. In the early spring of next year followed the procedures of squeezing, frying and storing up in mud for more than three years before it was ready for sale on the market. Jianhu Shaoxing Wine is one of the eight famous wines in China, the first registered trademark of Shaoxing Wine. Shaoxing Jianhu Brewery Lo., Ltd. is the first Shaoxing wine unit granted with the privilege of original product protection and a time-honored brand in China. It is also an industrial heritage protection base of the traditional brewing of Shaoxing Yellow Rice Wine.

遗产名称 / 位置：绍兴鉴湖黄酒作坊 / 浙江省绍兴市
Heritage item/Location: Shaoxing Jianhu Yellow Rice Wine Workshop/Shaoxing City, Zhejiang Province

浙江

鉴湖风光。佳酿之处必有名泉，绍兴黄酒因以鉴湖水酿造而闻名。
The scenery of Jianhu Lake. Where there is good wine, there is a famous spring. Shaoxing Yellow Rice Wine is famous for its source water of Jianhu Lake.

貳：核心物项
Section two: Core items

南大门、前大楼、后大楼等清代建筑，民国建筑西厢房，一组落作间、二组落作间、三组落作间、一组坛酒仓库、三组坛酒仓库、包装材料仓库等20世纪五六十年代建筑；鉴湖水取水口，原货物进出码头；瓦缸，瓦坛，木榨机，开耙工具，蒸饭木桶，专用弯斗，牌印；绍兴黄酒酿制技艺。

Buildings from Qing Dynasty such as the south gate, the front building and the back building, the west room built during the Republic of China, buildings in the 1950s and the 1960s such as the first group of rooms, the second group of rooms, the third group of rooms, the first group of altar wine warehouse, the third group of altar wine warehouse, packaging materials warehouse; water inlet of Jianhu Lake, the original pier; earthen jar, earthen altar, wood press machine, rake tool, steamed rice bucket, special bent bucket, brand seal; Shaoxing Yellow Rice Wine Brewing Technology.

清代壁画：位于南大门（清）明间柱楣上。
Murals in Qing Dynasty.

绍兴鉴湖黄酒作坊一直从酒药、麦曲制作开始，保持手工酿制的传统工艺精髓。从20世纪80年代起，黄酒作坊围绕黄酒生产中的蒸煮、放水、压榨、煎酒等工艺，进行技术设备改造提升。
Shaoxing Jianhu Yellow Rice Wine Workshop has always maintained handmade brewing starting from making Chinese yeast and wheat kojis. Since the 1980s, the workshop has upgraded the technical equipments for steaming and boiling, drainage, squeezing and decocting.

遗产名称/位置：绍兴鉴湖黄酒作坊/浙江省绍兴市
Heritage item/Location: Shaoxing Jianhu Yellow Rice Wine Workshop/Shaoxing City, Zhejiang Province

浙江

鉴湖酒坊大门。
The gate of Jianhu Yellow Rice Wine Workshop.

坛酒仓库（20世纪50年代）现用作黄酒存储仓库。
Altar wine warehouse (in the 1950s) is now used as a storage warehouse for yellow rice wine.

国家工业遗产
（第三批）

清代主体建筑三进，民国建筑一幢，20世纪六七十年代建筑六幢。
The main building with three courtyards in Qing Dynasty, one building in the Republic of China, 6 buildings in the 1960s to 1970s.

遗产名称/位置：绍兴鉴湖黄酒作坊/浙江省绍兴市
Heritage item/Location: Shaoxing Jianhu Yellow Rice Wine Workshop/Shaoxing City, Zhejiang Province

叁：遗产活化
Section three: Revitalization

　　绍兴鉴湖黄酒作坊地处绍兴黄酒小镇核心区域，已纳入绍兴市柯桥区规划的绍兴黄酒小镇北岸十里湖塘休闲区和黄酒文化旅游区。企业将遵循"原真保护、持续利用"原则，推进黄酒"产旅融合发展"，充分利用湖塘黄酒小镇开发的契机做好工业旅游，与大鉴湖风景旅游区相配套，进行参观体验、酿酒技艺展演、品鉴互动、餐饮购酒等项目，推进绍兴黄酒这一经典产业的振兴发展，彰显酒乡绍兴的文化底蕴与特色。

　　Located in Shaoxing Yellow Wine Town core area, Shaoxing Jianhu Yellow Wine Workshop has been incorporated into Shaoxing Yellow Wine Town north shore Shilihutang leisure area and Yellow Rice Wine cultural tourism area planned by Keqiao district, Shaoxing City.The company follows the principle of "all-round preservation and sustainable utilization" and makes full use of this opportunity to facilitate yellow rice wine production and its tourism industry. Together with Jianhu scenic tourism come such activities as field visit, wine-making skills show, taste and appreciation, catering and wine-shopping. Such efforts are made to revitalize Shaoxing yellow wine industry and highlight the wine town's culture and feature.

浙江

绍兴鉴湖黄酒作坊鸟瞰图。
Aerial view of Shaoxing Jianhu Yellow Rice Wine Workshop.

国家工业遗产（第三批）

古井贡酒年份原浆传统酿造区

千年制曲 献于庙堂
Distiller's Yeast with a Thousand Year's History, Wine Presented to Royal Court

壹：遗产春秋
Section one: History

古井贡酒的酿酒工艺起源于曹操向汉献帝进献九酝春酒及其酿造方法"九酝酒法"，距今有1 800多年的历史。
The wine-making process of Gujing Gong Wine traced back to over 1 800 years ago, when Cao Cao presented to Emperor Xian of Han Dynasty Jiuyunchun Wine and its brewing process.

古井贡酒酿造遗址公园国保区全景。
A panoramic view of the National Reserve— Gujing Gong Wine Brewing Relics Park.

遗产名称/位置：古井贡酒年份原浆传统酿造区/安徽省亳州市
Heritage item/Location: Traditional Brewing Area of Gujing Tribute Wine Original Pulp / Bozhou City, Anhui Province

古井贡酒酿造遗址是全国重点文物保护单位，包括宋井、明井、明清酿酒遗址、明清窖池群四个单体。在1958—2009年的四次考古发掘中，出土大量明中期至清代的酿酒和生活用品遗存，以及炉灶、排水沟、水井等酿酒文化遗存。

Gujing Gong Wine Brewing Relics has become a key national protection unit of cultural relics. It consists of wells from Song Dynasty, wells from Ming Dynasty, brewing relics from Ming and Qing Dynasties, and pits group from Ming and Qing Dynasties. In the four archaeological excavations from 1958 to 2009, a large number of wine-making and household remains from the Ming and Qing Dynasties were unearthed together with cultural remains as stoves, drainage ditches and wells.

古井贡酒酿造遗址是中国老八大名酒——"古井贡酒"产生、形成及发展的重要实物见证，具有重要的历史、科技、社会及艺术价值。

Gujing Gong Wine Brewing relics have witnessed the construction, formation and development of Gujing Gong Wine, one of the eight old-brand famous Chinese wines, and has important historical, scientific, social and artistic value.

安徽

贰：核心物项
Section two: Core items

宋井，明井，明代窖池群，清代窖池群，明清酿酒遗址，古井贡酒二号窖池群。

Wells from Song Dynasty, wells from Ming Dynasty, pits group from Ming Dynasty, pits group from Qing Dynasty, brewing relics from Ming and Qing Dynasties, the second pits group of Gujing Gong Wine.

宋代古井，作为文化景观对外展示。
The old well from Song Dynasty as the cultural sight for exhibition.

国家工业遗产（第三批）

明清窖池群，始建于明正德年间，距今已有500多年的历史，目前仍在继续使用。2013年5月，该遗址被列为全国重点文物保护单位，成为古井贡酒工业旅游、追溯中原地区酿酒工艺的极佳场所。
Pits group from Ming and Qing Dynasties. They were built in Zhengde period of Ming Dynasty and had an history of over 500 years. They are still in use. In May 2013, it was listed as a key national protection unit of cultural relics and therefore became an excellent place for industrial tourism and for knowing about the wine-making process of Central Plains.

遗产名称/位置：古井贡酒年份原浆传统酿造区 / 安徽省亳州市
Heritage item/Location: Traditional Brewing Area of Gujing Tribute Wine Original Pulp / Bozhou City, Anhui Province

安徽

酿酒工艺之分层取醅展示。
The presentation of distiller's grains in different layers.

叁：遗产故事
Section three: Craftsman

亳州，人文荟萃。明代末期（1643年），56岁的宋应星调任亳州知州，在当时"减酒"（古井贡酒前身）的浓香中，开启了他与亳州和古井贡酒的故事。

Bozhou is rich in humanities and talents. In the late Ming Dynasty (1643), the 56-years-old Song Yingxing was appointed as magistrate of Bozhou prefecture. Intoxicated in Jian Wine (the predecessor of Gujing Gong Wine), he started his story with Bozhou and Gujing Gong Wine.

宋应星痴迷于对万物之理的研究，在他履职亳州后，便对"公兴槽坊"所产的"减酒"（古井贡酒前身）爱不释手，开始从酒曲研究起酿酒技艺。宋应星在《天工开物》中对酒曲制作技艺也进行了详细描述，记载了麦曲制作方法——"曲为酒之骨"，制曲者"将麦连皮井水淘净，晒干"，然后在酒曲发酵期间，要经常查看酒曲的发酵情况，营造适宜酒曲发酵的环境等。由于制作酒曲对于工艺有着极高的要求，"故市曲之家必信著名闻"，才能不辜负出资酿酒的人。亳州所产的"减酒"曾数次作为贡品进献于庙堂。

Song Yingxing was obsessed with the study of the principle of all things. As he took office in Bozhou, he liked Jian Wine of "Gongxingcao brew house" so much that he took it with him all the time. And he began to study wine-making skills from making distiller's yeast. He described in full detail the yeast-making skills in his book *Exploitation of the Works of Nature*. He described how to make wheat yeast— essence of wine. Wash the wheat in "coat" with well water, dry them, start to ferment the yeast, have regular checks on the fermented yeast, and guarantee a suitable environment for wine fermentation. Because of the high standard in producing yeast, any famous brew house earned its reputation through building credibility so as to live up to the trust of the investor. Jian wine of Bozhou was presented to the royal court many times.

肆：遗产活化
Section four: Revitalization

古井集团依托质量科技园、酿造车间、现代化数字曲房等开发工业旅游。

Gujing Group develops industrial tourism relying on Quality science and Technology Park, brewing workshop and modern digital Qu room.

明清酿酒遗址。元末明初时期，吴国尚书郎怀叙后人从南京迁居减家店（今古井镇），以酿酒为生，怀氏后人对传统的"九酝酒法"进行改进，后称为"老五甑"工艺。在其带领下，此地酒坊林立，其中最著名的是"公兴糟坊"所产"减酒"。"公兴糟坊"即现今明清窖池及明清酿酒遗址所在地。

Brewing relics from Ming and Qing Dynasties. In the late Yuan Dynasty and early Ming Dynasty, a descendants of Huai Xu, the minister of Wu moved from Nanjing to Jianzhongdian (now known as Gujing Town) and made a living by making wine. Descendants of Huai family improved the traditional "nine-time glutinous rice fermenting" to "five-time distilling". Under their leadership, brew houses were found everywhere. Among the brew houses, the most famous one was "Gongxingcao brew house" producing Jian Wine. The location of "Gongxing Cao Brow House" is now known as the location of the pits group and brewing relics from Ming and Qing Dynasties.

国家工业遗产（第三批）

贵池茶厂

开创祁门红茶工业化新纪元
Create a New Era of Qimen Black Tea Industrialization

壹：遗产春秋
Section one: History

光绪元年（1875年），黟县人余干臣从福建罢官，回乡途中在至德（今池州东至县）尧渡街创制红茶成功。这成为祁门红茶的起源。

In the first year of Emperor Guangxu (1875), Yu Ganchen who was from Yi County dismissed from office in Fujian and returned his hometown. On his way home, he created a successful black tea at Yaodu Street in Zhide County (today's Dongzhi County in Chizhou City). This became the origin of Qimen Black Tea.

1950年，中国茶业公司皖南分公司开始在贵池县池口筹建大型新式机制茶厂——贵池茶厂。1951年，贵池茶厂正式建成。1984年，原贵池茶厂成为安徽省红茶唯一出口基地。2003年，贵池茶厂整体改制为安徽国润茶业有限公司。

In 1950, The Chinese Tea Company Wannan Branch began to build a large-scale new mechanism tea factory—Guichi Tea Factory in Chikou, Guichi County. In 1951, the construction of Guichi Tea Factory was formally completed, and in 1984, Guichi Tea Factory became the only export base of black tea in Anhui Province. In 2003, Guichi Tea Factory was wholly restructured into Anhui Guorun Tea Co., Ltd..

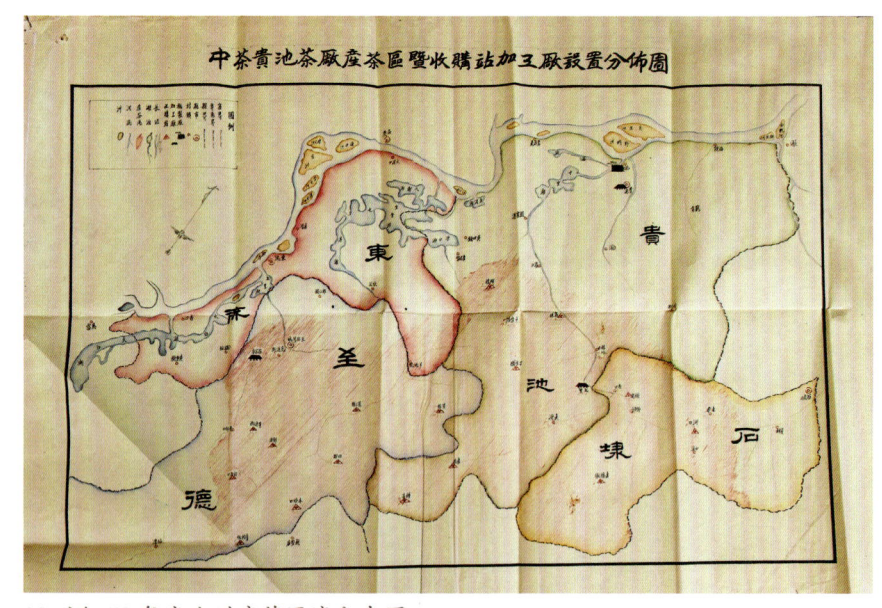

20世纪50年代池州产茶区域分布图。
Distribution map of Chizhou tea production regions in the 1950s.

遗产名称/位置：贵池茶厂/安徽省池州市
Heritage item/Location: Guichi Tea Factory / Chizhou City, Anhui Province

  贵池茶厂是新中国最早的祁门红茶生产加工企业，也是安徽省唯一保持了69年历史的茶叶企业，开创了世界级名茶祁门红茶工业化、标准化生产的历史新纪元。它见证了中国祁红产业乃至制茶工业的发展和变迁历程。

  Guichi Tea Factory is the earliest enterprise that produced and processed Qimen Black Tea in China, and also the only tea enterprise that has maintained a history of 69 years in Anhui Province, which initiated the historical epoch of industrialized and standardized production of Qimen Black Tea, a world-class famous tea. It witnessed the development and changes of China's Qimen Black Tea industry and even the whole tea production industry.

贰：核心物项
Section two: Core items

  祁红木仓，手工拣厂，精制茶车间及木质祁红生产线，拼配车间（外贸仓），包装车间，祁红审评大楼，办公楼，祁红加工培训场，职工之家；历史档案。

  Qimen Black Tea wooden warehouse, manual sorting factory, refined tea workshop and wooden Qimen Black Tea production line, assembly workshop (foreign trade warehouse), packaging workshop, Qimen Black Tea review building, office building, Qimen Black Tea processing training field, workers' home; historical archives.

抖筛工序。
Shaking and sifting process.

包装车间。整栋楼体始建于20世纪80年代末。最初是专为配套出口的原料加工车间。
Packaging workshop. The whole building was built in the late 1980s. Originally specially designed for supporting the export of raw materials processing workshop.

安徽

国家工业遗产（第三批）

　　祁门红茶的加工工艺包括初制的萎凋、揉捻、发酵、干燥和精制的抖筛、手筛、打袋、风选、飘筛、撼盘、手拣、拼配、补火、匀堆和装箱等步骤。这一套繁复的加工工艺已被列为非物质文化遗产。

　　Qimen Black Tea's processing technology includes preliminary's withering, rolling, fermentation, drying and refinement's shaking sift, hand sift, bag-beating, air selection, floating screen, tray, hand sorting, blending, fire filling, even piling and packing. This set of complicated processing technology has been listed as the Intangible Cultural Heritage.

祁红木仓内部。该枪中国茶叶界现存历史最久、规制最高、仍在使用的红茶木仓。
Inside of Qimen Black Tea wooden warehouse. It is the oldest existing black tea wooden warehouse in Chinese tea industry, with the highest regulation and still in use at present.

遗产名称/位置：贵池茶厂/安徽省池州市
Heritage item/Location: Guichi Tea Factory / Chizhou City, Anhui Province

安徽

手工拣厂。新中国成立初期建设的手工拣场整体为二层建筑，方形设计，苏式风格。最高峰时有1 200多人在拣厂工作。当年能在这里工作，是许多城市女性的梦想。
Hand sorting factory. The hand sorting factory constructed in the early period of founding of the People's Republic of China is a two-storey building with square design and Soviet-style. At its peaking period, more than 1 200 people were working in the hand sorting factory. It was the dream of many urban women to work here.

精制茶车间。这是一座锯齿形厂房，整体建筑呈苏式风格，是农产品转向国营化生产的见证物。
Refined tea workshop. This is a zigzag factory building, the overall construction is in the Soviet-style, and it is the evidence that witnesses agricultural products turning into the state-owned production.

国家工业遗产（第三批）

木质联装祁红生产线。采用大跨度设计，完全由56根空心廊柱支撑，形成无隔断墙的柱网空间，廊柱中空，便于雨天排水。
Qimen Black Tea wooden assembly production line. It adopts long span design, and is completely supported by 56 hollow columns, forming the column network space without partition wall. Hollow columns are convenient for drainage in the rainy days.

祁红木仓外部。
The outside of Qimen Black Tea wooden warehouse.

祁红加工培训场。非遗技艺传习所，始建于20世纪50年代，里面还存有当年制茶的各类设施设备，如萎凋槽、揉捻机、发酵室等。汪松柏、程晓祥等"红茶制作技艺非遗传承人"都曾在此学习。
Qimen Black Tea processing training field. The intangible cultural heritage skills transfer institute was built in the 1950s, which also stores the various facilities and equipment for tea production in the past, such as withering tank, rolling machine, fermentation room, etc. Wang Songbai, Cheng Xiaoxiang and other "the intangible cultural heritage inheritors of black tea production skills" had been here to learn.

祁红审评大楼。1985年4月,安徽省决定在贵池茶厂成立由祁红泰斗程家玉先生领衔的省祁门红茶审评检验小组,作为当时全省祁门红茶的权威审评机构在大楼内工作。
Qimen Black Tea review building. In April 1985, Anhui Province decided to set up the provincial Qimen Black Tea review and inspection team in Guichi Tea Factory and the Team was headed by Mr Cheng Jiayu, the master of Qimen Black Tea. It was the whole provincial authoritative review organization of Qimen Black Tea at that time.

国家工业遗产（第三批）

歙县老胡开文墨厂

传承千年的制墨技艺
Ink-making Technology Inherited for Thousands of Years

壹：遗产春秋
Section one: History

　　唐末，受安史之乱影响，制墨中心南移。南唐时期，全国制墨中心南移到歙县（古称歙州），自此开启了歙县千年制墨史。创建于1782年的歙县老胡开文墨厂是全国有名老字号。墨厂经历了1956年的徽墨业复兴潮、1961年的恢复桐油烟生产、1982年注册"李廷珪"商标，2003年企业改制等，制墨技艺也在不断传承与创新，制墨工艺由传承千年的家庭作坊演变为工厂生产。

　　At the end of the Tang Dynasty and affected by An-shi Rebellion, the national ink center moved south to She County (formerly known as She Zhou), and from then on She County had been making ink for thousands of years. Shexian Old Hu Kaiwen Ink Factory, found in 1782, was a famous time-honored brand in China. After such periods as Huizhou ink industry renaissance tide in 1956, resumed production of tung oil smoke in 1961, "Li Tinggui" trademark registration in 1982, and restructure in 2003, the ink making technology had been inherited and updated. Ink-making site changed from a family workshop to a factory.

每一块墨都是精美的艺术品，每一个墨模雕刻师都是集绘画、书法、雕刻、造型等于一体的工艺师。图为墨模雕刻师在模具制作车间雕刻墨模。
Each piece of ink is a fine work of art. Every ink mold sculptor is skilled at painting, calligraphy, sculpture and modeling. The picture shows a ink mold sculptor carving an ink mold in mold-making workshop.

遗产名称／位置：歙县老胡开文墨厂／安徽省黄山市歙县
Heritage item/Location:Shexian Old Hu Kaiwen Ink Factory/ She County Huangshan City Anhui Province

  2006年，歙县老胡开文墨厂"徽墨制作技艺"被国家和安徽省相继列入"第一批非物质文化遗产项目名录"，其现存的工业厂房、设备、技术及成果等，不仅体现了徽墨复兴历程，也见证了社会发展进程，成为一种"时代记忆"。
  In 2006, "Huizhou Ink-making Technology" of Shexian Old Hu Kaiwen Ink Factory was listed as "the first batch of intangible cultural heritage projects" by the state and Anhui Province successively. Its existing industrial plants, equipments, technology and achievements not only reflect the rejuvenation process of Huizhou Ink, but also witness the process of social development. It has become "memory of the times".

贰：核心物项
Section two: Core items

  生产车间3栋，古法点烟车间，办公楼，职工宿舍；点烟机、压墨机、搅坯机等生产设备，清同治年间模具（十大仙）10套；历史档案；徽墨制作技艺。
  3 production workshops, anancient lighting workshop, office building, staff dormitory; the production equipments such as lighter, ink press machine and billet mixing machine, 10 sets of molds (Ten Immortals) during the Reign of Emperor Tongzhi in Qing Dynasty; historical archives; Huizhou Ink-making Technology.

描金车间。描金是用金粉描绘出墨块上面的图案和文字，增加其观赏性。描金后的墨块晾晒12小时后，通过质检就是一块合格的徽墨了。
Gold tracing workshop. Gold tracing is to depict patterns and characters on the ink block with gold powder. After drying for 12 hours, the gold-traced ink block gets quality inspection, after which it becomes qualified Huizhou ink.

安徽

点烟机是炼烟的重要设备，烟灰是徽墨的主要原材料之一，炼烟使用的桐油均采于海拔1 600米左右，并且生长了3年以上油桐树果实压榨而成。经不完全燃烧，升起的烟雾经过收集管回收。

The lighter is an important equipment in refining smoke, Soot is one of the main raw materials of Huizhou ink.The tung oil used in smoke refining is squeezed out of the fruit of tung trees of over three-year-old and about 1 600 meters above sea level. From incomplete combustion of tung oil comes smoke rising intothe collection tube.

古法点烟，即灯盏碗烟。用桐油、猪油、生漆通过灯草燃烧。此炼烟法目前为制墨界独家生产，收集的烟加以动物皮胶、天然麝香、金箔、珍稀辅料及二十几味中药等调制，千锤百炼精制而成。古法油烟墨制作技艺为安徽省省级非物质文化遗产。

The ancient method of lighting is to use a bowl-shaped oil lamp. Tung oil, lard, raw lacquer are burned by lighting grass. This method of refining smoke is exclusive in the ink-making industry. After thoroughly tempered, the collected smoke, mixed with animal skin glue, natural musk, gold foil, rare auxiliary materials and more than 20 traditional Chinese medicines, is made into Huizhou ink.The ancient lampblack ink-making technology is the provincial intangible cultural heritage of Anhui province.

遗产名称 / 位置：歙县老胡开文墨厂 / 安徽省黄山市歙县
Heritage item/Location:Shexian Old Hu Kaiwen Ink Factory/ She County Huangshan City Anhui Province

安徽

晾墨车间。脱模之后要进行晾墨。晾墨室要保持恒温恒湿，避免阳光直射，风大要关窗，梅雨季要促进空气流通。晾墨要勤翻，以防墨坯收缩不匀而变形。

Ink drying workshop. After demoulding, the ink should be dried. Ink drying room should be of constant temperature and humidity and without direct sunlight. If it is windy, close the windows. In case of a rainy season, open the windows to facilitate ventilation. Turnink blank over frequently to avoid deformation from uneven shrink.

碾压机。粗糙结块的墨泥，一遍遍经过机器的碾轧，变得细腻润泽。之后将墨泥做成饼状，送往制墨车间。

Rolling machine. After rolling over and over again by the machine, the rough ink chunk becomes smooth and moist.Then the ink chunk is shaped into paste and sent to the ink-making workshop.

20世纪70年代建成的工厂办公楼。
The office building built in the 1970s.

遗产名称/位置：歙县老胡开文墨厂/安徽省黄山市歙县
Heritage item/Location:Shexian Old Hu Kaiwen Ink Factory/ She County Huangshan City Anhui Province

胡开文
Hu Kaiwen

　　胡开文（1742—1808），墨业的创始人，原名胡天柱，字柱臣，号在丰，清代四大徽墨家之一。乾隆三十年（1765年），承顶汪启茂墨店，为制作高质量产品，挑选旧墨模中之精品，不惜巨资购买上等原料，聘良工刻模制墨，并取徽州府孔庙的"天开文苑"金匾中间两字，打出"胡开文墨庄"店号，在竞争中独占鳌头。

Hu Kaiwen (1742—1808), founder of ink industry, was one of the four Huizhou ink masters of Qing Dynasty. His former name is Hu Tianzhu, with a styled name of Zhuchen and an assumed name of Zaifeng. In the 30th year of Qianlong's reign (1765), he took over Wang Qimao Ink Shop. In order to produce high-quality ink, he chose the best old ink molds, spared no expense to buy the best raw material, and hired veterans to make ink molds. In addition, he took the middle two Chinese characters in the plaque of "Tian Kai Wen Yuan" in Confucius Temple of Huizhou and renamed its shop as "Hu Kaiwen Ink Workshop", which came out first in the field.

　　胡天柱的次子胡余德，于乾隆四十七年（1782年）创胡开文墨店。清末，"胡开文"这块招牌被出租，甚至招股或卖招牌。于是，各地陆续出现外姓人开的"胡开文"墨店，甚至有人混淆视听。后来，胡家人为了证明自身的正宗改名为"老胡开文"。

Hu Tianzhu's second son, Hu Yude, founded "Hu Kaiwen" ink shop in the 45th year of Qianlong' reign (1782). At the end of the Qing Dynasty, the brand of "Hu Kaiwen" was rented out and even came out for sale. "Hu Kaiwen" ink shops opened by people of other surnames appeared in various places. Later on, descendants of Hu family changed their name to "Old Hu Kaiwen" to identify themselves.

十大仙墨模。"十大仙"墨模是清同治年间墨模高手王绥之的得意之作，为歙县老胡开文墨厂珍藏的孤版。为保护历史名模，限量生产。1977年"十大仙墨"首次在美国销售，受到华侨和美国爱好徽墨人士及收藏家的欢迎与厚爱。

Ten Immortals Ink Molds. The "ten immortals" ink molds were the masterpiece of Wang Suizhi, a master of ink mold in the period of Emperor Tongzhi in Qing Dynasty. It's a unique edition of ink mold treasured by She County Old Hu Kaiwen Ink Factory. In order to protect these molds, the factory sets a limit on the production of "ten immortal" ink. In 1977, "ten immortal" ink was first launched for sale in the United States. They were welcomed and loved by overseas Chinese, American ink lovers and collectors.

安徽

国家工业遗产（第三批）

泉州源和堂蜜饯厂

源和堂蜜饯承载甜蜜记忆
Yuanhetang preserves carry sweet memories

壹：遗产春秋
Section one: History

泉州源和堂蜜饯厂的前身是始建于1916年的庄氏兄弟蜜饯作坊，采用古法腌制工艺生产的果干，味道甜美。源和堂的牌号与制作配料"盐"和"糖"暗合，寓意精妙，距今已有上百年历史。源和堂蜜饯厂曾是泉州工业发展史上的三大典型代表，员工最多时达数千人。

Quanzhou Yuanhetang Candied Fruits Factory was formerly known as Zhuang Brothers Candied Fruit Workshop established in 1916. They adopted an ancient method in making candied fruit, which was delicious and digestive. Its brand name "Yuanhetang" is an homo-phonic pun, with "Yuan" for "Yan"—Chinese sound of "salt" and "tang" — Chinese pronunciation of "sugar". As both salt and sugar are essential ingredients of candied fruit, the brand provokes a profound conception. With a history of hundreds of years and thousands of employees at most, it was one of the three typical representatives in Quanzhou industrial history.

泉州源和堂蜜饯厂入厂大门。
The gate of Quanzhou Yuanhetang Candied Fruits Factory.

遗产名称/位置：泉州源和堂蜜饯厂/福建省泉州市鲤城区
Heritage item/Location: Quanzhou Yuanhetang Candied Fruits Factory/Licheng District, Quanzhou City, Fujian Province

　　泉州源和堂蜜饯厂是福建省国有企业泉州中侨（集团）股份有限公司下属的三大厂房之一。2011年，泉州源和堂蜜饯厂"修旧如旧"，在坚持保留工业遗产记忆的基础上，改造成集"创意设计、文化艺术、旅游休闲"于一体的源和1916创意产业园。在转型发展的同时，泉州源和堂蜜饯厂完整保留了一批20世纪50年代至80年代具有闽南特色和工业遗产记忆的石头建筑、闽南瓦片、车间、仓库、食堂、烟囱等重要建筑和景观。目前该园区既是国家"AAAA"级旅游景区，也是福建省首批创意产业重点园区之一，入驻文创类企业200多家。

Quanzhou Yuanhetang Candied Fruits Factory is one of the three plants subordinate to Quanzhou Zhongqiao (Group) Co., Ltd., a state-owned enterprise in Fujian Province. In 2011, Quanzhou Yuanhetang Candied Fruits Factory renovated the factory with the best effort to maintain its original look. It was transformed into Yuanhe 1916 Creative Industrial Park themed as "creative design, culture and art, tourism and leisure" on the basis of preserving and representing the industrial heritage. During the period of transformation, Quanzhou Yuanhetang Candied Fruits Factory had completely retained a batch of important buildings and sights with Minnan characteristics and of the industrial heritage memory from the 1950s to the 1980s, such as stone buildings, Minnan tiles, workshops, warehouses, canteens, and chimneys. At present, the park is not only a national "AAAA" tourist attraction, but also one of the first key parks of creative industry in Fujian Province with over 200 cultural and creative enterprises.

源和堂相关老照片。Related old photos of Yuanhetang.

源和堂冰糖车间。Yuanhetang crystal sugar workshop.

福建

贰：核心物项
Section two: Core items

蜜饯腌制池，蜜制车间，10吨锅炉房、6吨锅炉房、饮料生产车间、冰糖大楼（含冰糖车间和蜜饯晒场），白糖仓库，包装车间和成品仓库，厂大门，地磅，办公楼，行政办公室，员工食堂；蜜饯汤汁浓缩罐，蜜饯搅拌机、搅拌棍、晾晒拨勺，蜜饯腌制缸、晾晒簸箕；历史照片12件套，《泉州中侨》期刊一套。

Candied fruits preserved pool, syrup curing workshop, 10-ton boiler room, 6-ton boiler room, beverage production workshop, crystal sugar building (including crystal sugar workshop and candied fruits airing yard), sugar warehouse, packaging workshop and finished product warehouse, factory gate, truck scale, office building, administrative office, staff canteen; candied fruit juice condensed tank, candied fruit mixer, mixing sticks, airing scoops, candied fruits curing jars, airing dustpans; 12 sets of historical photos, one set of periodicals named *Quanzhou Zhongqiao*.

源和堂航拍图。
The aerial photo of Yuanhetang.

遗产名称/位置：泉州源和堂蜜饯厂/福建省泉州市鲤城区
Heritage item/Location: Quanzhou Yuanhetang Candied Fruits Factory/Licheng District, Quanzhou City, Fujian Province

蜜饯晾晒簸箕。
Airing dustpan.

源和堂大烟囱。
Yuanhetang big chimney.

源和堂蜜饯晒场。
Yuanhetang candied fruits airing yard.

福建

国家工业遗产（第三批）

源和堂包装车间和成品仓库。
Yuanhetang packaging workshop and finished product warehouse.

遗产名称 / 位置：泉州源和堂蜜饯厂 / 福建省泉州市鲤城区
Heritage item/Location: Quanzhou Yuanhetang Candied Fruits Factory/Licheng District, Quanzhou City, Fujian Province

叁：遗产活化
Section three: Revitalization

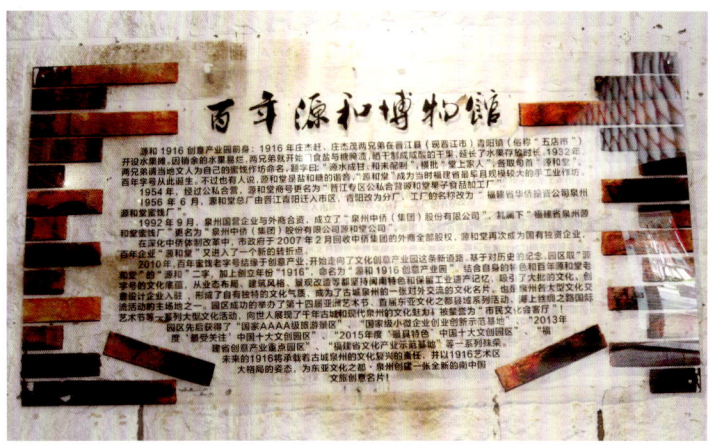

百年源和博物馆：记录源和 1916 年至今的工业记忆。
Centennial Yuanhe Museum: recording industrial memories of Yuanhe from 1916 till now.

源和 1916 孵化楼。
Yuanhe 1916 incubator building.

福建

国家工业遗产（第三批）

福建红旗机器厂

从容烽火路 浓浓军工情
The Military Factory behind the Self-defense War

壹：遗产春秋
Section one: History

　　红旗机器厂，1970年年底，一座始建于20世纪60年代末的国家中型军工厂在闽西长汀县馆前镇东阳山东济岩的群山中悄然形成，共完成了50多栋厂房、2.5千米的厂区公路、水坝供水系统、变电站和长1 000多米、总面积5 000多平方米的两大人工开凿洞体，适宜生产、分散、隐蔽，洞口能防御1 000磅炸弹的直接命中。

　　Hongqi Machinery Factory, At the end of 1970, a national medium-sized military factory under construction since the late 1960s came to shape in the mountainous area of Dongji cliff, Dongyang range, Guanqian Town, Changting County, west of Fujian Province. The project included over 50 plants, 2.5 kilometers of factory roads, dam water supply system, transformer substation and 2 artifical tunnels. Each tunnel was about 1 000-meter-long and covered a total area of over 5 000 square meters, suitable for production, dispersal, concealment, and defense against a 1000-pound-bomb attacking.

　　20世纪70年代初，工厂开始12.7毫米高射机枪的试制生产工作。1972年11月29日，五四式12.7毫米高射机枪正式转为大批量生产。1973年的生产能力为年产150挺，1975年达到了年产500挺的技术水平。到了1978年，福建红旗机器厂以超出设计规模两倍产量的优异的成绩，实现了"一厂顶二厂"的宏伟目标，被国家授予"大庆式企业"荣誉称号。尤其在对越自卫反击战中，12.7毫米高射机枪屡建奇功，摧毁敌方暗堡、山洞枪眼无数，深受前沿部队青睐，得到了国防部的表扬，创造了军品时期的光辉业绩。

　　In the early 1970s, the Fujian Red Flag Machine Factory began to make 12.7mm anti-aircraft machine guns, and on November 29th, 1972, Wusishi 12.7mm anti-aircraft machine gun was officially put into mass production. Its annual production capacity was 150 in 1973, and amounted to 500 in 1975. In 1978, Fujian Red Flag Machine Factory had a production capacity twice of the original goal and made such achievement as one factory functioning as two. It was awarded by the state the title of "Daqing-style Enterprise". Especially in the self-defense war against Vietnam, 12.7mm anti-aircraft machine guns had done an outstanding job in destroying the enemy's bunkers despite countless embrasures. The gun earned the favor of vanguards, got the praise of the Ministry of Defense and created a glory in the military period.

遗产名称 / 位置：福建红旗机器厂 / 福建省龙岩市长汀县
Heritage item/Location: Fujian Red Flag Machine Factory/ Changting County, Longyan City, Fujian Province.

"北有香山红叶，南有东阳红枫"。遗址周围山体树木和自然景观得到很好的保护，厂区内栽种了红豆杉、银杏、樱花等上万棵珍贵树种。遗址所处的长汀县东阳山大峡谷是优美的原生态山地景观，是闽西名山之一。

"Northern Xiangshan Mountain is best-known for its red leaves, while southern Dongyang Mountain is famous for its red maple." The trees on the mountain and natural landscape around the relic are well preserved. Tens of thousands of precious trees such as taxus chinensis, ginkgo and sakura have been planted in the factory. The Grand Canyon of Dongyang Mountain in Changding County is a beautiful ecological mountain landscape and one of the famous mountains of western Fujian Province.

大礼堂。
Auditorium.

福建

贰：核心物项
Section two: Core items

厂房，办公楼，大礼堂，宿舍楼，商店，食堂，澡堂，医院，幼儿园，学校，灯光球场，人工开凿洞体。
Plants, office building, auditorium, dormitory buildings, store, canteen, bathhouse, hospital, kindergarten, school, lamp court, artificial tunnel.

食堂旧址。
The Old Mess Hall.

遗产名称 / 位置：福建红旗机器厂 / 福建省龙岩市长汀县
Heritage item/Location: Fujian Red Flag Machine Factory/ Changting County, Longyan City, Fujian Province.

在对越自卫反击战中，红旗机器厂制造的12.7毫米高射机枪屡建奇功。
The repeated achievement of 12.7mm anti-aircraft machine guns made by Fujian Red Flag Machine Factory in the self-defense war against Vietnam.

20世纪70年代的车间。
Plants in the 1970s.

福建

福建红旗机器厂航拍全景图。
An aerial photo of the panoramic view of Fujian Red Flag Machine Factory.

125

叁：遗产活化
Section three: Revitalization

七层岩。
Seven-layer-cliff.

厂区自然风光
Landscape in the factory.

国家工业遗产（第三批）

景德镇明清御窑厂遗址

御器声华蜚万国　窑炉风火越千年
The Flame of Kilns Burns for Thousands of Years

壹：遗产春秋
Section one: History

景德镇明清御窑厂遗址是能全面、系统反映我国官窑陶瓷生产和文化信息的历史遗存。它建于明洪武二年（1369年），结束于清宣统三年（1911年），历经明清两代26位皇帝，为皇帝烧造御瓷长达542年。

Jingdezhen Ming-and-Qing Imperial Kiln Factory Site is a historical heritage that can reflect the ceramic production and culture of the royal kiln in a comprehensive and systematic way. It was built in the second year of Hongwu of Ming Dynasty (1369), and closed in the third year of Xuantong in Qing Dynasty (1911). It operated for 542 years and served 26 emperors of Ming and Qing Dynasties.

景德镇明清御窑厂遗址大门。
Gate of Jingdezhen Ming-and-Qing Dynasty Imperial Kiln Factory Site.

明御窑瓷厂遗址。
Ming Dynasty Imperial Kiln Factory Site.

| 遗产名称/位置：景德镇明清御窑厂遗址/江西省景德镇市 |
| Heritage item/Location: Jingdezhen Ming-and-Qing Dynasty Imperial Kiln Factory Site/Jingdezhen City, Jiangxi Province |

现存遗址及其背景环境是研究景德镇御窑厂历史沿革、管理制度、烧造工艺的重要依据，也是研究历史文化名城景德镇城市发展脉络的重要基础，对全世界陶瓷业的发展做出了不可磨灭的贡献，在世界范围内具有不可替代的历史、科学和艺术价值。御窑厂是景德镇制瓷业发展到巅峰时期的产物，是景德镇瓷文化的突出代表，也代表了当时世界手工业的最高水平，在中国及世界手工业史上具有特殊的地位。

The existing site and its background circumstance are key to the study of historical evolution, management system and firing craft of Jingdezhen Royal kiln factory, and that of the progress of the famous historical and cultural city—Jingdezhen. It has made an indelible contribution to the development of porcelain industry all over the world, and has irreplaceable historical, scientific and artistic value in the world. Imperial Kiln Factory came into shape at the peak period of Jingdezhen porcelain industry and stood as outstanding representative of Jingdezhen porcelain culture. It represented the highest level of the handicraft industry in the world at that time, and possessed a special status in the history of handicraft industry at home and abroad.

贰：核心物项
Section two: Core items

明清时期御窑厂窑业遗迹（含窑炉遗迹、作坊遗迹），墙体、道路遗迹，古井、古树，窑业堆积遗迹，衙署建筑及其他附属建筑遗迹，与明清御窑紧密相关的元代官窑遗迹，出土御窑遗物。

Relics of kiln factories in Ming and Qing Dynasties (including kiln relics, workshop relics), wall, road relics, ancient well, ancient trees, kiln-related relics, government buildings and other ancillary buildings relics, imperial kiln relics of Yuan Dynasty closely related to the imperial kiln in Ming and Qing Dynasties, unearthed relics of imperial kiln.

古井。由麻石堆砌而成，可以看出麻石材料的坚固，井深17米，底下还有水井口是圆形，里面是方形的，就像古代铜钱的形状，也有天圆地方宇宙观的体现。

Ancient well. The ancient well is made of solid granite which can reflect the firm of solid granites. The ancient well is 17 meters deep. The well mouth is round and the inside is square, just like the shape of ancient copper coins, which also reflects the cosmological view of round sky and square earth.

明清作坊遗址。
Workshops relics in Ming and Qing Dynasties.

明代马蹄窑遗址。
Site of Ming Dynasty Horseshoe Kiln.

明代葫芦窑遗址。
Site of Ming Dynasty Hulu Kiln.

明代御器厂东北角围墙遗址。
Ming Dynasty Imperial Furniture Factory Northeast corner of the wall site.

遗产名称/位置：景德镇明清御窑厂遗址/江西省景德镇市
Heritage item/Location: Jingdezhen Ming-and-Qing Dynasty Imperial Kiln Factory Site/Jingdezhen City, Jiangxi Province

江西

御窑厂国家考古遗址公园。
Imperial Kiln Factory National Archaeological Remains Park.

中国御窑工艺博物馆。
China Imperial Kiln Craft Museum.

国家工业遗产（第三批）

龙珠阁。景德镇地标性的建筑，始建于唐代，在唐代的时候叫聚珠亭，1990年重建，2013年翻新。
Long Zhu Pavilion. Long Zhu Pavilion is a landmark building in Jingdezhen. It was first built in Tang Dynasty and named as Ju Zhu Pavilion. It was rebuilt in 1990 and renovated in 2013.

遗产名称/位置：景德镇明清御窑厂遗址/江西省景德镇市
Heritage item/Location: Jingdezhen Ming-and-Qing Dynasty Imperial Kiln Factory Site/Jingdezhen City, Jiangxi Province

江西

街巷。南北为街，东西为弄，条条里弄通长江。街巷格局形成于宋元。
Street-and-alley. The north-south road is called street, the east-west road is called alley, and every alley leads to the Yangtze River. The street-and-alley pattern was formed in Song and Yuan Dynasties.

国家工业遗产（第三批）

景德镇国营为民瓷厂

新中国景德镇陶瓷工业历史的重要见证
The Important Witness of Jingdezhen Ceramic Industry in China

壹：遗产春秋
Section one: History

景德镇国营为民瓷厂位于世界瓷都景德镇，为"十大瓷厂"之一，筹建于1957年11月，曾经是全国38家大中型重点企业之一，江西省出口瓷主要生产企业，景德镇市新花瓷生的产主要基地。

Jingdezhen State-owned Weimin Porcelain Factory, located in the global porcelain center —Jingdezhen and founded in November 1957, was among the "top ten porcelain factories" and one of the 38 large-and-medium-sized key enterprises in China. It is the main porcelain enterprise for export in Jiangxi Province, and the main producer of Xinghua porcelain in Jingdezhen City.

景德镇国营为民瓷厂以生产出口新彩杯碟和高级美术瓷而闻名于世，其产品集实用与艺术于一体，出口港澳地区和欧美、东南亚市场，深受国内外客户喜爱。其设计生产的接待美国前总统尼克松的《兰牡丹金菊盖杯》（尼克松杯）、前苏联领导人戈尔巴乔夫的戈氏西餐具，为瓷厂赢得了巨大国际声誉和效益。

Jingdezhen State-owned Weimin Porcelain Factory is famous for producing and exporting new color cups and saucers and delicate decorative ceramics. Its products with both practical and artistic values are exported to Hong Kong and Macao, Europe, America and Southeast Asia, and win the favor of both domestic and foreign customers. The blue peony cup with gold chrysanthemum lid (Nixon Cup) designed for receiving former President of the United States Richard Nixon and Gorbachev tableware produced for receiving former Soviet leader Mikhail Gorbachev have enjoyed great international reputation and have gained profound profit for the porcelain factory.

景德镇国营为民瓷厂充分重视文化建设，1977年4月，响应党中央"工业学大庆""普及大庆式企业"的号召，按大庆式企业的标准进行内部整顿，全面落实岗位责任和经济责任，被江西省委、省政府授予"大庆式企业"称号，成为全陶瓷系统第一家。景德镇国营为民瓷厂自办《为民报》，组织技术人员编印《日用陶瓷工艺》教材向全国发行。

Attaching importance to cultural construction, in April 1977, in response to the call of the CPC Central Committee to "learn from Daqing industry" and to "popularize Daqing type enterprise", Jingdezhen State-owend Weimin Porcelain Factory carried out internal reorganization in accordance with Daqing type enterprise standards, fully implemented post responsibility and economic responsibility, and became the first ceramic enterprise awarded the title of "Daqing-type Enterprise" by Jiangxi Provincial Party Committee and provincial government. Jingdezhen State-owend Weimin Porcelain Factory ran its own newspaper *Weimin Daily* and organized technicians to compile and print the teaching material *Ceramic Technology for Daily Use* which was issued nationwide.

遗产名称/位置：**景德镇国营为民瓷厂** / 江西省景德镇市
Heritage item/Location: Jingdezhen State-run Weimin Porcelain Factory/Jingdezhen City, Jiangxi Province

贰：核心物项
Section two: Core items

原料车间，成型二车间、三车间，琢器车间、彩绘车间、辊道窑、白胎仓库，红花仓库，倒焰窑厂房，隧道窑厂房，成品仓库，配电车间，模型车间，锅炉房，厂大门，行政办公楼，工会大楼，职工食堂，放映厅，烟囱，太湖石；发电机、砂轮、喇叭口、漏斗等生产工具；老照片、证书、奖状、书籍等历史档案。

Raw material workshop, the second molding workshop, the third workshop, carving workshop, painting workshop, roller kiln, white base warehouse, safflower warehouse, down-draft kiln workshop, tunnel kiln workshop, finished product warehouse, distribution workshop, model workshop, boiler room, factory gate, administrative offices buiding, union building, staff canteen, video hall, chimney, Taihu lake stones; production tools such as generator, grinding wheel, flared mouth and funnel; historical archives such as old photos, certificates, awards and books.

景德镇国营为民瓷厂以生产出口新彩杯碟和高级美术瓷闻名于世，是中国景德镇陶瓷工业辉煌历史的重要见证。
Jingdezhen State-owned Weimin Porcelain Factory is famous for producing and exporting new color cups and saucers and delicate decorative ceramics. It witnesses the glorious history of Jingdezhen ceramic industry in China.

国家工业遗产（第三批）

景德镇国营为民瓷厂厂房俯瞰。
Aerial view of Jingdezhen State-owned Weimin Porcelain Factory.

136

遗产名称/位置：**景德镇国营为民瓷厂** / **江西省景德镇市**
Heritage item/Location: Jingdezhen State-run Weimin Porcelain Factory/Jingdezhen City, Jiangxi Province

车间内部。
The interior of a workshop.

烟囱。
The chimney.

叁：遗产活化
Section three: Revitalization

景德镇陶瓷工业遗产博物馆内生产设备展示。
Production equipment displayed in Jingdezhen Ceramic Industrial Heritage Museum.

景德镇陶瓷工业遗产博物馆内部。
Interior of Jingdezhen Ceramic Industrial Heritage Museum.

倒焰窑。19世纪50年代，位于景德镇陶瓷工业遗产博物馆内。景德镇陶瓷工业遗产博物馆利用宇宙瓷厂内留存的旧窑房，通过修补、修复创新，打造出独特的文化体验空间，游客可以通过馆内一系列展览，了解景德镇近现代陶瓷工业的变迁发展。

The down-draft kiln. It was built in the 1950s, and located in Jingdezhen Ceramic Industrial Heritage Museum. The Museum created a unique space for cultural experience by revamping and innovating the old kiln workshops of the Universe Porcelain Factory and constructing such iconic cultural landscapes. Visitors can learn about the changes and evolvement of Jingdezhen's modern ceramic industry through a series of exhibitions.

国家工业遗产（第三批）

吉州窑遗址

拥有1 200年历史的古民窑遗址
Ancient min kiln site with a history of 1 200 years

壹：遗产春秋
Section one: History

  吉州窑是我国古代江南地区一座综合性民间窑场，创烧于晚唐，兴于五代、北宋，极盛于南宋，距今已有1 200年的历史。2001年，吉州窑被国务院列为国家重点文物保护单位。吉州窑8万平方米的窑区里约有72.6万立方米的陶片堆积，保存的从晚唐至宋元时期的24座窑包是目前世界上发现规模最庞大，保存最完整的古民窑遗址群。

  With a history of 1 200 years, Jizhou Kiln is a comprehensive folk kiln factory in Jiangnan area of ancient China. It originated in the late Tang Dynasty, flourished in the Five Dynasties and the Northern Song Dynasty, and peaked in the Southern Song Dynasty. In 2001, Jizhou Kiln was listed as a key cultural relic protection unit by the State Council. About 726 000 cubic meters of ceramic shards are deposited in the 80 000-square-meter Jizhou Kiln area. The 24 kilns preserved from the late Tang Dynasty to the Song and Yuan Dynasties are the largest and most complete ancient kiln ruins found in the world.

吉州窑的古建筑（古窑址、古道观、古街、古村、古祠、古巷）。
The historic buildings of Jizhou Kiln (the ancient kin site, Taoist temple, street, village, Ancient temple and alley).

遗产名称/位置：吉州窑遗址/江西省吉安市吉安县
Heritage item/Location: Jizhou Kiln Site/Ji'an County,Jian City,Jiangxi Province

吉州窑产品种类繁多，风格多样，已发现120多种，其制作工艺精湛，特色鲜明，以黑釉瓷和彩绘瓷最负盛名，是吉州窑瓷器的典型代表。黑釉瓷中木叶天目盏、剪纸贴花、窑变釉纹等产品更是"器走天下"，誉满世界，被世界上多个国家列为国宝级文物进行收藏。吉州窑的釉下彩绘技艺，对此后景德镇青花瓷的产生影响极大。

Jizhou Kiln has a wide variety of products and various styles. More than 120 kinds of them have been discovered. With exquisite workmanship and distinctive features, Jizhou kiln is best known for its black glaze porcelain and painted porcelain, which is a typical representative of Jizhou Kiln porcelain.The products of black glazed porcelain, such as Mu Ye Tian Mu glaze tea cup, paper-cut decals and flambe glazedporcelain, are well known all over the world and are collected as national historical relics in many countries in the world.The underglaze painting technique of Jizhou Kiln has a great influence on the blue and white porcelain of Jingdezhen.

贰：核心物项
Section two: Core items

本觉寺龙窑遗址，茅庵岭遗址，丹砂渡古码头遗址；24个古窑包；木叶天目盏、剪纸贴花、彩绘瓷等出土文物；吉州窑匣钵古道，制瓷作坊遗址。

Benjue Temple Longyao site, ruins of Maoanling, Danshadu Ancient wharf site; 24 ancient kilns ; Unearthed cultural relics such as Mu Ye Tian Mu glaze tea cup, paper-cut decals and painted porcelain; Jizhou Kiln sagger ancient road, ruins of porcelain workshop.

吉州窑茅庵岭遗址于2014年2月—2015年2月进行挖掘，揭露面积2 100平方米，发现龙窑两座、房屋一座、匣钵道路一条等，出土了大量宋、元、明的青白釉、白釉、绿釉瓷、黑瓷、釉下彩绘等瓷器标本。

From February 2014 to February 2015, the excavation of ruins of Jizhou Kiln Maoanling was carried out, covering an area of 2 100 square meters. Two pieces of dragon kiln, one house, one sagger road were found. A large number of blue and white glaze, white glaze, green glaze, black porcelain, underglaze painting and other porcelain specimens of Song, Yuan and Ming Dynasties were unearthed.

国家工业遗产
（第三批）

吉州窑出土文物：木叶天目盏。
Cultural relics unearthed at Jizhou Kiln: Mu Ye Tian Mu glaze tea cup.

南宋吉州窑木叶纹盏。内外均施黑釉，盏内放一片桑叶，送入窑室烧制。在经过1 300摄氏度高温之后，这片桑叶不仅没有灰飞烟灭，相反，其美丽的纹路、形体、脉络永恒而完整无缺地保留在了漆黑的茶盏上。吉州窑木叶天目盏是将"一叶一菩提"的禅文化推向极致的经典之作。
Southern Song Dynasty Jizhou Kiln Mu Ye Wen glaze tea cup. Black glazes are applied inside and outside the ware, and a mulberry leaf is put in the cup and sent to the kiln for firing. After 1300 degrees, the mulberry leaf not only did not disappear, on the contrary, its beautiful lines, shapes and veins remained eternally and intact in the dark tea cup. Jizhou Kiln Mu Ye Tian Mu glaze tea cup is the classic work that pushes the Zen culture of "one leaf and one Bodhi" to the extreme.

北宋吉州窑红绿釉印花纹盏。
Jizhou Kiln red and green glaze printing pattern cup in the Northern Song Dynasty.

吉州窑出土文物。
Cultural relics unearthed at Jizhou Kiln.

遗产名称/位置：吉州窑遗址/江西省吉安市吉安县
Heritage item/Location: Jizhou Kiln Site/Ji'an County,Jian City,Jiangxi Province

吉州窑匣钵古道，古代路面遗迹。用匣钵砌成，属于明清时期的遗址。
Jizhou Kiln sagger ancient road is a relic of ancient road. The road was paved by saggers in Ming and Qing Dynasties.

老陶瓷厂作坊遗址。2012年9月—11月考古挖掘共清理釉缸等28处遗迹，出土了一批宋、元、明的青白釉、白釉、绿釉瓷、黑瓷、釉下彩绘的瓷器标本。
Ruins of the ancient ceramic workshop. From September 2012 to November 2012, archaeological excavations were carried out a total of 28 remains such as glaze jars were cleaned up. A large number of blue and white glaze, white glaze, green glaze, black porcelain, underglaze painting porcelain specimens of Song, Yuan and Ming Dynasties were unearthed.

江西

叁：遗产活化
Section three: Revitalization

遗产名称/位置：吉州窑遗址/江西省吉安市吉安县
Heritage item/Location: Jizhou Kiln Site/Ji'an County,Jian City,Jiangxi Province

吉州窑特色小镇的特色项目：洗茶体验。
Special event of Jizhou kiln characteristic town: tea washing experience.

江西

中国吉州窑博物馆。2012年启动建设，2015年2月26日正式对外开放，是目前唯一一家展示吉州窑的专题博物馆。
China Jizhou Kiln Museum. The museum started construction in 2012 and was officially opened to the public on February 26th, 2015. It is currently the only museum dedicated to displaying Jizhou Kiln.

国家工业遗产（第三批）

兴国官田中央兵工厂

人民军工发祥地　传承强军首责精神

The Birthplace of People's Military Industry, Taking Army Reinforcement as Priority

壹：遗产春秋
Section one: History

兴国官田中央兵工厂位于江西省赣州市兴国县兴莲乡官田村，是中国共产党创办的第一个大型综合性兵工厂。1931年秋，兵工厂第一代领导人吴汉杰受中革军委的委派筹建中央红军总部直属修械所，10月根据毛泽东、朱德的指示，中革军委命令红军总部白石修械所、红三军团修械所与江西省苏维埃政府修械所合并，在官田宣告成立兵工厂。

Xingguo Guantian Central Military Factory is located in Guantian Village, Xinglian Township, Xingguo County, Ganzhou City, Jiangxi Province, and it is the first large-scale comprehensive military factory founded by the Communist Party of China. In the autumn of 1931, Wu Hanjie, the first generation of leader of the military factory, was appointed by the Central Revolutionary Army Commission to build a mechanic institute directly subordinate to Central Red Army headquarters. In October 1931, according to the instructions of Mao Zedong and Zhu De, the Chinese Central Military Commission ordered the Red Army headquarters white stone mechanic institute to merge with the third Red Army mechanic institute and Jiangxi Province Soviet governmental mechanic institute to establish Guantian military factory.

兴国官田中央兵工厂在驻设官田两年半的时间里，共修配了四万多支步枪，生产了四十多万发子弹，修理了两千多挺机枪、百余门迫击炮、两门山炮，造了六万多枚手雷、五千多个地雷，丰富了红军的军事装备，对打击敌人、赢得革命战争的胜利发挥了重要作用。

In the two-and-a-half years in Guantian, Xingguo Guantian Central Military Factory assembled and repaired a total of over 40 000 rifles; fixed over 400 000 rounds of ammunition, repaired more than 2 000 machine guns, over 100 mortars and 2 pieces of artillery; made over 60 000 hand grenades and over 5 000 mines. All these enriched the Red Army's military arms and played a key role in winning the victory of revolutionary war.

兴国官田中央兵工厂不仅述说了老一代兵工人"不忘初心，牢记强军首责"的精神，更奠立了我国工业企业的发展基石。

Xingguo Guantian Central Military Factory not only witnessed the contribution of our old generation of soldiers and workers to build a strong army, but also laid the cornerstone for the development of China's industrial enterprises.

遗产名称 / 位置：兴国官田中央兵工厂 / 江西省赣州市兴国县
Heritage item/Location: Xingguo Guantian Central Military Factory/ Xingguo County, Ganzhou City, Jiangxi Province

贰：核心物项
Section two: Core items

总务科（厂部）旧址，弹药科旧址，枪炮科旧址，利铁科旧址，俱乐部旧址，护厂特务连旧址；10 马力发电机、30 马力发电机、手摇钻床、手摇冲压机、车床等生产设备原件；历史档案。

Original site of general affairs section (headquarter), original site of ammunition section, original site of gun and mortar section, original site of iron production section original site of the club, original site of special agent factory-guarding company; original producing equipments as 10 horsepower generator, 30 horsepower generator, hand-drilling machine, band-punch, and lathe; historical archives.

江西

官田中央兵工厂旧址。
Old site of Guantian Central Military Factory.

国家工业遗产（第三批）

总务科旧址内部。
Inside of original site of general affairs section.

总务科旧址始建于清代晚期。1931年10月，中央兵工厂总务科驻此，作为总厂办公厅。
The original site of general affairs stction was built in the late Qing Dynasty. In October 1931, it became the headquarter of general affairs section of Central Military Factory.

遗产名称 / 位置：兴国官田中央兵工厂 / 江西省赣州市兴国县
Heritage item/Location: Xingguo Guantian Central Military Factory/ Xingguo County, Ganzhou City, Jiangxi Province

江西

弹药科旧址内部。
Inside of original site of ammunition section.

弹药科旧址。始建于清康熙年间，1931年10月中央兵工厂弹药科驻此。
Original site of ammunition section. It was builted in Kangxi period of Qing Dynasty. In October 1931, it became the ammunition section of Central Military Factory.

国家工业遗产（第三批）

历史档案资料。
Historical archives.

枪炮科旧址始建于清顺治年间。1931年10月中央兵工厂枪炮科驻此。
Original site of gun and mortar section was built in Shunzhi period of Qing Dynasty. In October 1931, it became the gun and mortar section of Central Military Factory.

利铁科旧址内部。
Inside of original site of iron production section.

利铁科旧址始建于1924年，干打垒土木结构。1931年10月中央兵工厂利铁科（含杂械科）驻此。
The original site of iron production section was built in 1924 with an adobe construction. In October 1931, it became the iron production section(including mechanic section) of Central Military Factory.

150

遗产名称/位置：兴国官田中央兵工厂 / 江西省赣州市兴国县
Heritage item/Location: Xingguo Guantian Central Military Factory/ Xingguo County, Ganzhou City, Jiangxi Province

叁：遗产活化
Section three: Revitalization

兴国官田中央兵工厂致力于打造官田军工特色小镇。图为利铁科工人蜡像。
Xingguo Guantian Central Military Factory is committed to build a featured town of military industry. The photo shows the waxen image of workers of iron production section.

生产设备原件。Original producing equipments.

江西

国家工业遗产（第三批）

潍坊大英烟公司

浓缩中国百年烟草工业发展史
Epitome of A-hundred-year History of Chinese Tobacco Industry

壹：遗产春秋
Section one: History

潍坊大英烟公司始建于1917年，毗邻胶济铁路廿里堡车站，总占地面积340亩，建筑面积6万平方米，是国内目前规模大、保存完整的烟叶复烤厂。

Weifang Daying Tobacco Company was founded in 1917, near Nianlipu Station of Jiaoji Railway. With a total area of 340 Mu (10 hectares) and a construction area of 60 000 square meters, the factory is a large-scale and well-preserved tobacco re-drying plant.

近百年来，潍坊大英烟公司在烤烟技术传承、推动技术变革等方面做出了突出贡献。潍坊大英烟公司是科学技术的产物，无论是厂房设施，还是机器设备，无一不代表了当时最为先进的科学技术水平，是一个时期展示工业科学、技术科学、建筑科学的重要窗口之一，浓缩了中国烟草工业及山东省烟草加工的发展史。

In the past century, Weifang Daying Tobacco Company has made outstanding contributions to the inheritance of tobacco technology and the promotion of technological innovation. Weifang Daying Tobacco Company was the product of science and technology. Whether its plant facilities or machinery and equipment, all represented the most advanced science and technology at that time. It was one of the important showpiece of industrial science, technical science, architectural science of a certain period as well as an epitome of development history of Chinese tobacco industry and Shandong Province's tobacco processing.

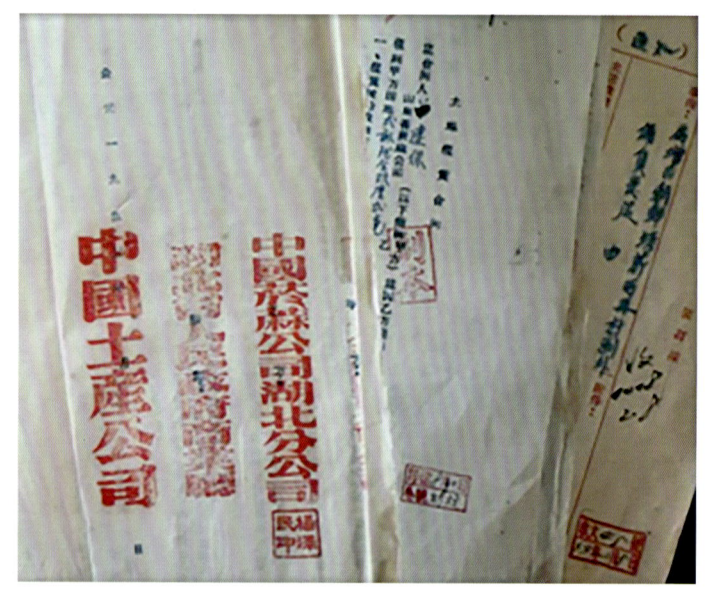

历史档案。
Historical archives.

遗产名称/位置：潍坊大英烟公司/山东省潍坊市
Heritage item/Location: Weifang Daying Tobacco Company/ Weifang City, Shandong Province

阅读链接 Link for further reading

百年红色地道群
A-century-old Tunnels

1917年，潍坊大英烟公司创建时期，各库房、办公区下都建有逃生地道，主干道高1.8米、宽1.5米。1945年，国民党行政第八区行署将烟厂改建为兵营，并将地面地堡工事与地下坑道连通。

In 1917, Weifang Daying Tobacco Company is built with escaping tunnels in its warehouses and office buildings, with the main line 1.8 meters high and 1.5 meters wide. In 1945, Administrative Office of the 8th District of the Nationalist Party revamped the factory into a barrack and connected the above-ground bunker fortifications with the underground tunnels.

地道群内部。
Inside of the tunnels.

新中国成立初期，地道开挖部分用于战备防护。到了20世纪60年代，在加固扩充部分原有老地道的基础上，烟厂工人按照战备防空的要求，修建了地下指挥部、蓄水池等民防设施，完成北厂环线贯通后与南厂地道群相连。

In the early period of the People's Republic of China, tunnel entrance was used for shelter against war. By the 1960s, workers of the tobacco factory reinforced and expanded some of the original tunnels, and built such civil defense facilities as underground headquarters and reservoirs in line with the requirements of defense against war. In this way, ring road of north plant was connected with the tunnel complex of the south plant.

2017年，这一庞大的百年地道群被发现，已经探明的地道总长度近6千米，目前成为爱国主义教育基地。

In 2017, this large-scale, 100-year-old tunnel complex was discovered, with a total length of nearly 6 kilometers. It is now a patriotic education base.

山东

贰：核心物项
Section two: Core items

烟叶复烤车间，东小洋楼，西小洋楼，账房，1号储烟库，2号储烟库，1—16号仓库，1—15码垛基座，工业和消防用400立方米蓄水池（2.5米×9米×18米）、总长约6千米的战备逃生地道群，历史档案。

Tobacco re-drying workshop, east western-style building, west western-style building, accounting room, No.1 tobacco warehouse, No.2 tobacco warehouse, No.1 to No.16 warehouses, No.1 to No.15 pallet base, 400 cubic meters of reservoir (2.5 meters × 9 meters × 18 meters) for industrial and fire-fighting usage, defense tunnel complex of a total length of about 6 kilometers, historical archives.

华人账房共13间，由英、美亲信的买办负责，统辖管理华人职工事宜。
Chinese accounting rooms, 13 rooms all together. Pro-Anglo and pro-American are in charge of accounting rooms and responsible for Chinese workers management.

户外烟草储备基座，始建于新中国成立初期。
Outdoor tobacco reserve base, built in the early period of the People's Republic of China.

烟叶复烤车间。
Tobacco re-drying workshop.

储烟库。
Tobacco warehouse.

遗产名称 / 位置：潍坊大英烟公司 / 山东省潍坊市
Heritage item/Location: Weifang Daying Tobacco Company/ Weifang City, Shandong Province

典型西欧式建筑。由于平面呈零式飞机形，也被称为"飞机楼"，为英、美高层商务代表办公、居住使用。
Typical Western European-style architecture. Because the flat surface is shaped like a z-plane, it is also known as "aircraft building". It is the business office and residence for British and American executives.

国家工业遗产（第三批）

叁：遗产活化
Section three: Revitalization

　　2017年，在保留潍坊大英烟公司旧址工业风格的基础上，以保护性利用为主线，相关方将遗址项目打造为文化创意、科普教育、爱国主义、研学教育融合发展基地——潍坊1532文化产业园，搭建文、商、旅、居、学综合发展的文创产业聚集区，成为山东省精品文化旅游和爱国教育文化基地。

　　In 2017, Weifang Daying Tobacco Company relic was revamped into Weifang 1532 Cultural Industrial Park with the purpose of revitalizing the relic on the basis of best preservation of its industrial style. The park combined cultural creativity with science popularization, patriotism and research and education to build a cultural industry center of culture, business, travel, residence and learning, also a fine cultural tourism and patriotic educational and cultural base of Shandong Province.

改造后的户外烟草储备基座、储烟库、烟叶复烤车间、库房等。
Revamped outdoor tobacco reserve base, tobacco warehouse, tobacco re-drying workshop, warehouse etc.

遗产名称 / 位置：潍坊大英烟公司 / 山东省潍坊市
Heritage item/Location: Weifang Daying Tobacco Company/ Weifang City, Shandong Province

山东

小洋楼。
Western-style building.

国家工业遗产（第三批）

东阿阿胶厂78号旧址

寿人济世　使命传承
Benefiting Mankind and Prolonging Life-span, Participating in its Inheritance

壹：遗产春秋
Section one: History

　　东阿阿胶厂建于1952年，其原型是创立于嘉庆五年的同兴堂。同兴堂是近代上清阿胶炼制技艺的集大成者，因创立"九九炼胶法"而名声大震。东阿阿胶厂78号旧址始建于1969年，是东阿阿胶股份有限公司2013年之前的主要生产区。该工业遗址记载着阿胶行业乃至中医药行业许多历史性的瞬间，见证了新中国成立以来东阿阿胶厂坚守初心、革故鼎新的奋斗历程，以及其将"寿人济世"作为企业使命的发展与传承。

　　Dong'e Ejiao Factory was established in 1952 and formerly known as Tongxing Tang found in the fifth year of Jiaqing. Tongxing Tang was the master of pure Ejiao refining techniques in modern times, and gained great fame for the establishment of "Nine days and nine nights, and ninety-nine procedures of refining Ejiao". Built in 1969, the original site of Dong'e Ejiao Factory No.78 was the main production area for Dong'e Ejiao Co., Ltd. until 2013. The industrial site recorded many historic moments in the Ejiao industry and even the traditional Chinese medicine industry. It witnessed Dong'e Ejiao Factory's pursuit of its original aspiration and successive innovation; also it saw the inheritance of the factory's mission—"benefiting mankind and prolonging life-span".

东阿阿胶厂原厂区大门。
The gate of original Dong'e Ejiao Factory.

20世纪阿胶生产中的手工熬胶场景。
A scene of refining Ejiao by hand in the 20th century.

遗产名称/位置：东阿阿胶厂 78 号旧址/山东省聊城市
Heritage item/Location: the original site of Dong'e Ejiao Factory No.78/Liaocheng City, Shandong Province

贰：核心物项
Section two: Core items

原料处理车间，阿胶生产楼，琉璃井，糖浆剂生产楼，冷冻站，擦胶包装楼，复方阿胶浆生产车间，仓库大楼，综合办公楼；EH-4 蒸球化皮机，脚踏式切胶机，机械自动切胶机，小型压盖机，颗粒包装机，卧螺离心机，生产设备及工具 19 件套；1966 年东阿牌商标注册证等历史档案。

Raw material processing workshop, Ejiao production building, coloured glaze well, syrup production building, refrigeration station, Ejiao wiping and packaging building, compound Ejiao pulp production workshop, warehouse building, comprehensive office building, EH-4 steamed ball-shaped melting donkey hide machine, pedal Ejiao cutting machine, automatic mechanical Ejiao cutting machine, small capping machine, granule packing machine, horizontal screw centrifuge, 19 sets of production equipments and tools, Dong'e brand trademark registration certificatein in 1966 and other historical archives.

东阿阿胶厂 78 号旧址。
The original site of Dong'e Ejiao Factory No.78.

国家工业遗产
（第三批）

脚踏式切胶机。
Pedal Ejiao cutting machine.

国内第一台 EH-4 蒸球化皮机。
The first EH-4 steamed ball-shaped melting donkey hide machine in China.

1986年，东阿阿胶厂自主研制出机械自动切胶机，标志着切胶工艺进入机械化生产时代。
In 1986, Dong'e Ejiao Factory independently developed an automatic mechanical cutting machine, entering into mechanized production.

遗产名称/位置：东阿阿胶厂78号旧址/山东省聊城市
Heritage item/Location: the original site of Dong'e Ejiao Factory No.78/Liaocheng City, Shandong Province

叁：遗产活化
Section three: Revitalization

　　目前，东阿阿胶厂78号旧址整体保留完整，部分区域在保留原貌的基础上改造成了阿胶文化主题酒店，实现了新旧动能转换，为东阿阿胶股份有限公司开展工业旅游提供了重要支撑。

　　At present, the original site of Dong'e Ejiao Factory No.78 is well preserved, part of which has been converted into an Ejiao Culture Theme Hotel. After the transformation, it has fundamentally supported the industrial tourism of Dong'e Ejiao Co., Ltd..

阿胶文化主题酒店。
Ejiao Culture Theme Hotel.

国家工业遗产（第三批）

湖北 5133 厂

创造军工奇迹的火箭炮制造基地
A Rocket-making Base that Creates a Military-industrial Miracle

壹：遗产春秋
Section one: History

湖北 5133 厂（江山重工研究院）曾经的"江山机械厂"，是我国"三线火箭炮总装厂旧址"。20 世纪 60 年代，根据中共中央将生产力布局由东向西战略大调整的三线建设战略，按照"靠山、分散、隐蔽"方针，江山机械厂于 1969 年 4 月在湖北襄阳开始了其筚路蓝缕的创业之路。400 多平方米的带锯房，从设计到施工，从设备安装到调试生产，只用了 1 个月。1969 年年底，江山机械厂便装配出了第一门 107 火箭炮，并在武汉进行了展览，余秋里、张连奎等中央领导驻足观看，赞叹工厂创造了"当年定点、当年产出"的军工奇迹。

5133 Factory of Hubei Province (namely Jiangshan Heavy Industry Research Institute) used to be "Jiangshan Machinery Factory" is the former site of Third-Front Rocket Launcher Assembly Plant in China. In the 1960s, according to the three-line construction strategy of the CPC Central Committee to adjust the distribution of productivity from east to west, Jiangshan Machinery Factory began its entrepreneurial path in April 1969 in Xiangyang City, Hubei Province, in accordance with the principle of "deep in the mountain, scattered and concealed". It took only one month to design and complete constructing the sawing room of more than 400 square meters, including installing and adjusting the equipment for production. At the end of 1969, Jiangshan Machinery Factory assembled the first 107 rocket gun, which was exhibited in Wuhan. Central leaders as Yu Qiuli, Zhang Liankui took a good look at the gun and applauded the factory for creating a military miracle of "starting to produce and finishing in the same year".

从 1969 年到 1979 年，江山机械厂基本完成第一期工程建设，并形成了一定的生产能力，4 个型号的火箭炮产品先后投入生产。此后，江山犹如雄鹰展翅，为年轻的共和国增添了一处稳固的兵器工业基地，成为我国在鄂西北地区兴建的大型军工企业。如今，公司累计向部队提供各式火箭炮、布雷车等武器设备 2 000 多门（份），荣获国家级、省部级科技进步奖 50 余项，多次参加国庆及建军阅兵大典。

From 1969 to 1979, Jianshan Machinery Factory completed the first phase of construction. It had certain production capacity with 4 models of rocket gun put into operation. Since then, Jiangshan Heavy Industry was like an eagle flying high in the sky; it was a solid weapons industry base to the People's Republic of China and became a large-scale military enterprise in northwest of Hubei Province. Till now, the company has provided to the troops more than 2 000 pieces of weapons, for instance, all kinds of rockets, vehicles and other weapons and equipments. It has won more than 50 national, provincial and ministerial prizes for progresses in science and technology. The weapons and equipment produced by the factory were exhibited in the military parade of the National Day many a time.

遗产名称 / 位置：湖北 5133 厂 / 湖北省襄阳市老河口市
Heritage item/Location: 5133 Factory of Hubei Province / Laohekou, Xiangyang City, Hubei Province.

江山重工研究院，这支隶属中国兵器工业集团，位于华中腹地、汉水之滨的兵工劲旅，历经五十多年风雨坎坷，从三线建设的艰辛、保军转民的奋争、创新发展的探索，如今已成为我国重要的火箭炮武器科研生产制造基地、国防科技工业双保军企业。

Jiangshan Heavy Industry Research Institute, located in the hinterland of Central China at the coast of Hanshui, is a strong force of China's Weapon Industry Group. After more than 50 years of ups and downs from Third-Front construction, military-to-civilian service transformation, to exploration for innovative development, it has become China's important research and production base of rocket gun weapons and a double-guarantee military enterprise in national defense science and technology industry.

湖北 5133 厂早起制造的火箭炮。
Early rocket made by 5133 Factory of Hubei Province.

湖北

国家工业遗产（第三批）

贰：核心物项
Section two: Core items

建设指挥部，北办公楼，301工房，302工房，305工房，铁路专用线，工人俱乐部，招待所，溜冰场，篮球场；车床等机床16台/套，滚齿机，插齿机，圆刻线机，剪板机，长刻线机，投影仪，光切显微镜。

Construction headquarter, north office building, 301 workshop, 302 workshop, 305 workshop, special railway line, Workers' Club, guest house, ice rink, basketball court; 16 sets of lathe and other machine tools, hobbing machine, gear shaping machine, circular dividing machine, shearing machine, long ruling engine, projector, light-section microscope.

铁路专用线。
Special railway line.

遗产名称 / 位置：湖北 5133 厂 / 湖北省襄阳市老河口市
Heritage item/Location: 5133 Factory of Hubei Province / Laohekou, Xiangyang City, Hubei Province.

部分机床设备。
Part of machine tool equipments.

工房内景。
Inside of workshop.

湖北

国家工业遗产
（第三批）

厂区老招待所。
Old guest house.

江山工人俱乐部。
Jiangshan Workers' Club.

遗产名称/位置：湖北 5133 厂 / 湖北省襄阳市老河口市

Heritage item/Location: 5133 Factory of Hubei Province / Laohekou, Xiangyang City, Hubei Province.

叁：遗产今夕
Section three: Current Situation

今天，江山重工研究院的襄阳江山科技园、老河口基地"一厂三区" 总体布局日益完善；创新江山、质量江山、精益江山、数字江山、幸福江山建设全面推进。江山重工研究院将聚焦装备研发和技术研究体系建设，对标世界一流，坚决履行强军首责，奋力推动企业高质量发展，在"五型江山"建设的宏伟征程上阔步前行。

Today, Jiangshan Heavy Industry Research Institute overall layout of "one factory three parks"—Xiangyang Jiangshan Science and Technology Park, Old Estuary Base begin to take shape. Constructions of innovative Jiangshan, quality Jiangshan, refine Jiangshan, digital Jiangshan, happiness Jiangshan are promoted in an all-round way. Jiangshan Heavy Industry Research Institute will focus on equipment R&D and technology research system construction, benchmarking world-class, firmly fulfill the first responsibility of strengthening the army, strive to promote the high-quality development of enterprises, and stride forward on the grand journey of "five type Jiangshan" construction.

江山重工研究院厂区现状。
Current situation of Jiangshan Heavy Industry Research Institute.

湖北

国家工业遗产（第三批）

华新水泥厂旧址

中国水泥行业的教科书
A Textbook of China's Cement Industry

壹：遗产春秋
Section one: History

华新水泥厂旧址地处湖北省黄石市黄石港区，占地面积约 5.4 万平方米，是我国现存时代较早、保存规模最大、最完整的水泥工业遗产，填补了我国近代水泥工业遗产保护的空白。

Huaxin Cement Factory is located in Huangshigang District, Huangshi City, Hubei Province, covering an area of about 54 000 square meters. It is the oldest, largest and most complete cement industrial relic, filling a gap in modern cement industrial heritage protection in China.

华新水泥厂旧址是我国近代最早开办的三家水泥厂之一，原名大冶湖北水泥厂，创建于 1907 年。1946 年 9 月 28 日，在现址兴建了华新水泥股份有限公司大冶水泥厂。1949 年年初，第一台湿法水泥窑建成投产。1950 年，华新水泥股份有限公司和大冶水泥厂合并，后经社会主义公有制改造成为华新水泥厂。2005 年起，华新水泥厂老厂区陆续停产。2007 年 7 月 19 日，这个百年老厂关停了最后一组水泥生产线。

Huaxin Cement Factory was founded in 1907, formerly known as Daye Hubei Cement Factory, one of the three earliest cement factories in modern China. On September 28th, 1946, Daye Cement Factory of Huaxin Cement Co., Ltd. was built at the present site. At the beginning of 1949, the first wet cement kiln was completed and put into operation. In 1950, Huaxin Cement Co., Ltd. merged with Daye Cement Factory, and after the reconstruction of socialist public ownership, it was transformed into Huaxin Cement Factory. Since 2005, old plants of Huaxin Cement Factory was discontinued in a roll. On July 19th, 2007, the century-old plant closed its last set of cement production line.

华新水泥厂旧址见证了中国水泥工业从萌芽、发展到走向现代的历史进程，是功能建筑与设计的代表作，更是中国水泥行业的教科书，曾被毛泽东誉为"远东第一"。2013 年，华新水泥厂旧址被国务院公布为第七批全国重点文物保护单位，包括 7.39 万平方米设施、83 个文物单元。

Huaxin Cement Factory has witnessed the historical process of China's cement industry from germination, development to modernization. It is not only a representative work of functional architecture and design, but also a textbook of China's cement industry. It was once honored as "the first in the Far East" by Mao Zedong. In 2013, Huaxin Cement Factory was listed by the State Council in the seventh batch of National Key Cultural Relic Protection Units, including 73 900 square meters of facilities and 83 cultural relic units.

遗产名称/位置：华新水泥厂旧址/湖北省黄石市
Heritage item/Location: Former site of Huaxin Cement Factory/Huangshi City, Hubei Province

阅读链接 Link for further reading

华新之最
The "most" of Huaxin

华新水泥厂旧址现存三台大型水泥湿法旋窑。其中，1、2号窑始建于1946年，系从美国爱立斯公司原装引进的两条大型水泥湿法旋窑和配套设备，这是目前世界上仅有保存完好的湿法水泥旋转窑设备。3号窑由华新人自主设计建造，1977年正式投产，代表了当时我国水泥工业的先进水平，并出口20多条生产线，被命名为"华新窑"，成为中国水泥工业的里程碑。

There are three large cement wet rotary kilns at Huaxin Cement Factory. Among them, No. 1 kiln and No. 2 kiln were built in 1946 and are two large cement rotary kilns with their supporting equipments originally introduced from Ellis Company in the United States. They are the only well-preserved rotary cement kilns in the world. No. 3 kiln was designed and built by Huaxin people independently and put into operation in 1977, which represented the advanced level of China's cement industry at that time. It exported more than 20 production lines and was named "Huaxin kiln", becoming a milestone of China's cement industry.

湖北

华新水泥厂旧址全景
Panoramic view of Huaxin Cement Factory

贰：核心物项
Section two: Core items

卸石坑，联合储库，厚浆池，储浆池，1—3号湿法回转窑，2 000吨水泥库，包装车间。

Unloading pit, joint storage, thick slurry tank, slurry storage tank, No.1 to No.3 wet rotary kilns, 2 000-ton cement warehouse, packaging workshop.

厚浆池。
The thick slurry tank.

联合储库。
The joint storage.

包装车间。
The packaging workshop.

遗产名称/位置：华新水泥厂旧址/湖北省黄石市
Heritage item/Location: Former site of Huaxin Cement Factory/Huangshi City, Hubei Province

叁：遗产活化
Section three: Revitalization

作为民族水泥工业的骄傲，华新水泥厂旧址已被改造成水泥博物馆。
As the pride of the national cement industry, Huaxin Cement Factory has been transformed into a cement museum.

车间旧址。
The former site of workshops.

湖北

中核二七二厂铀水冶纯化生产线及配套工程

核工业继承发展的活态遗产
A Living Legacy of the Nuclear Industry

壹：遗产春秋
Section one: History

中核二七二厂，始建于1958年，是"一五"计划期间建设的156项重点工程项目之一，是我国第一座工艺流程完善、能处理多种矿石和生产多种铀产品的大型铀水冶纯化厂，曾为我国"两弹一艇"的研制成功做出积极贡献。

272 Plant of CNNC, founded in 1958, is one of 156 key engineering projects constructed during "the first Five-Year Plan" period. It is China's first large-scale uranium hydrometallurgy and purification plant with perfect technological process, capable of processing a variety of ores and producing various uranium products. It has made positive contributions to the successful development of "A-bomb, H-bomb and nuclear-powered submarine" in China.

中核二七二厂办公楼外景。
Exterior view of the office building of 272 Plant of CNNC.

遗产名称/位置：中核二七二厂铀水冶纯化生产线及配套工程/湖南省衡阳市
Heritage item/Location: 272 Plant of CNNC Uranium hydrometallurgy and Purification Production Line and Supporting Projects/Hengyang City, Hunan Province

1958年创建至今，中核二七二厂先后历经了三次历史阶段的时代沉浮，不断地积累和发展，并且在新时期面临着更大的发展机遇，致力于打造百年老厂，所以中核二七二厂的工业遗产是核工业继承发展的活态遗产。二七二铀纯化生产线目前仍是我国唯一一条工艺成熟、技术可靠、已工程化处理国产铀化学浓缩物的生产线。中核二七二厂的发展历程见证了我国核工业的历史变迁，是核工业精神的典型代表，具有典型的核军工特色和国防教育意义。

Since its establishment in 1958, the constantly developing 272 Plant of CNNC has experienced three historical ups and downs. Seizing the opportunity of the new period, the plant was committed to building a century-old plant and becoming a living legacy of the nuclear industry. At present, the 272 uranium purification production line is still the only one in China with mature technology, reliable technology and engineering treatment of domestic uranium chemical concentrate. 272 Plant of CNNC, with typical nuclear military characteristics and significance of national defense education, witnesses the development of China's nuclear industry and represents the spirit of the nuclear industry.

阅读链接 Link for further reading

中核二七二厂厂风
Factory Style of 272 Plant of CNNC

"四个一切"核工业精神，一直是中核二七二厂自力更生、攻坚克难、摆脱困境、创新发展、勇攀高峰的坚强支撑和不竭动力。

The "four everything" spirit of nuclear industry has always been the strong support and inexhaustible driving force for 272 Plant of CNNC to be self-reliant, overcome difficulties, get rid of difficulties, innovate and develop, and scale new heights.

一次创业期间（1962年）颁布了"勤、紧、细、稳、准、慎"的六字厂风。

During the first period of business establishment (1962), the six-character factory style of "diligence, tightness, delicacy, stability, accuracy and prudence" were promulgated.

二次创业期间（1983年）制定了"团结、求实、严细、创新"的八字厂风。

During the second entrepreneurial period (1983), the four-character work style of "united, practical, meticulous and innovative" was formulated.

改革发展新时期（2016年），丰富发展了"融"文化体系，明确了"融"文化构成，即"融愿、融志、融心、融德"四个部分，即企业使命，做国际铀纯化转化技术发展的引领者；企业愿景，强核强国、造福人类；企业精神，"两弹一星"精神、"四个一切"核工业精神；企业核心价值观：责任、安全、创新、协同。

In the new period of reform and development (2016), the system of "harmony" culture has been enriched and developed, and it has been clarified that "harmony" culture consists of four parts, namely, harmony of will, harmony of aspiration, harmony of heart and harmony of virtue. To lead the development of international uranium purification and conversion technology has become the mission of the plant. To be a strong nuclear power and benefit mankind is the corporate vision. The spirit of "two bombs and one satellite" and the spirit of "four everything" constitute the enterprise spirit. Corporate core values: responsibility, safety, innovation and coordination.

湖南

贰：核心物项
Section two: Core items

铀纯化老生产线，铀水冶生产线，铀尾矿库，铁路专用线和蒸汽机火车头，高射炮，江边泵房。

Old production line for uranium purification, uranium hydrometallurgical production line, uranium tailings impoundment, special railway line and steam engine locomotive, anti-aircraft gun, river-side pump house.

建厂初期，中核二七二厂属于一级保密单位，警卫营配置高射炮用作空中防御。20世纪80年代，警卫营撤离，高射炮移交给中核二七二厂武装部。

In the early days of its establishment, 272 Plant of CNNC was a first-class security unit, and the guards battalion was equipped with anti-aircraft guns for air defense. In the 1980s, the battalion left the plant and the anti-aircraft guns were handed over to the Armed Personnel Division of 272 Plant of CNNC.

负责铀矿石及专业原料运送的二七二铁路专用线，1962年投入运行，总长 13 876.95 米。

In charge of transporting uranium ore and professional raw materials, the 272 railway special line put into operation in 1962, with a total length of 13 876.95 meters.

中核二七二厂铀尾矿库是铀水冶纯化生产线重要的配套工程，始建于1958年，1995年进入退役治理程序。目前，铀尾矿库形成了占地面积约170万平方米，九个坝段与三个丘陵山头围拦而成的平地型尾矿库，是中国第一铀尾矿库。

The uranium tailings impoundment of 272 Plant of CNNC is an important supporting project for the production line of uranium hydrometallurgy and purification. It was built in 1958 and decommissioned in 1995. At present, the uranium tailings impoundment has formed a flatland type tailings impoundment with an area of about 1.7 million square meters. It is the first uranium tailings impoundment in China, surrounded by nine dam sections and three hills.

遗产名称/位置：中核二七二厂铀水冶纯化生产线及配套工程/湖南省衡阳市
Heritage item/Location: 272 Plant of CNNC Uranium hydrometallurgy and Purification Production Line and Supporting Projects/Hengyang City, Hunan Province

衡阳铀水冶厂球磨机。
Ball grinders of Hengyang Uranium Hydrometallurgical Plant.

中核二七二厂建厂26周年纪念碑。
Monument to the 26th anniversary of 272 Plant of CNNC.

中核二七二厂曾被称为衡阳铀水冶厂，于1963年建成铀水冶生产线，是我国第一座工艺流程完善，能处理多种矿石和生产多种铀产品的水冶厂。
272 Plant of CNNC, once known as Hengyang Uranium Hydrometallurgical Plant, completed its uranium hydrometallurgical production line in 1963. It is China's first hydrometallurgy plant with perfect technological process, capable of processing a variety of ores and producing various uranium products.

湖南

叁：遗产活化
Section three: Revitalization

  2007年，中核二七二厂军品部分从母体中剥离出来，正式成立中核二七二铀业有限责任公司，成为中核集团南北两个铀纯化转化生产基地之一，继续为国防建设和核电发展做出贡献。

  In 2007, the military product of 272 Plant of CNNC was separated from its parent plant, and CNNC 272 Uranium Limited Liability Company was formally established. It has become one of the two uranium purification and conversion production bases in the north and south of CNNC, and continues to make contributions to national defense construction and nuclear power development.

  在保护和利用方面，中核二七二厂打造了传承广场，将铀水冶生产线的流程、关键设备实物还原展示，在保持工业遗产原真性和完整性的同时，打造主题广场和企业展馆，对内教育员工，对外开展爱国主义和国防教育，构建展示平台，助推企业发展和核工业文化传播。

  In terms of protection and utilization, 272 Plant of CNNC has built an Inheritance Square to display the production line of uranium hydrometallurgical and its key equipments. The Inheritance Square and enterprise pavilions, while maintaining the authenticity and integrity of the industrial heritage, provide a platform for carrying out patriotism and national defense education both in and out of the company, and promote the development of the company and the spread of nuclear industry culture.

传承广场。
Inheritance Square.

遗产名称/位置：中核二七二厂铀水冶纯化生产线及配套工程/湖南省衡阳市
Heritage item/Location: 272 Plant of CNNC Uranium hydrometallurgy and Purification Production Line and Supporting Projects/Hengyang City, Hunan Province

湖南

传承广场。
Inheritance Square.

国家工业遗产（第三批）

南风古灶 ★★★

沿用至今的最古老柴烧龙窑
The Oldest Wood Fired Dragon Kiln in Using up to Now

壹：遗产春秋
Section one: History

南风古灶和高灶是明代建造用于烧制陶艺作品和日用陶产品的柴烧龙窑，距今有500年历史。南风古灶全长34.4米，窑背上有29排火眼，具有保存完好、持续使用时间长的特点。高灶全长32.7米，结构与南风古灶一致，目前仍保持每月烧窑两次的使用频率。2001年，两条龙窑成为第五批全国重点文物保护单位，南风古灶更以"连续使用至今的最古老柴烧龙窑"的名义载入"大世界基尼斯"之最。

With a history of 500 years, Nanfeng Ancient Stove and High Stove are wood fired kilns built in Ming Dynasty for firing pottery works and daily ceramic products. Nanfeng Ancient Stove is 34.4 meters long and has 29 rows of fire holes on the back of the kiln. It is well preserved and lasts for a long time. The High Stove is 32.7 meters in length and has the same structure as Nanfeng Ancient Stove. At present, it is still firing twice a month. In 2001, two kilns became the fifth batch of National Key Cultural Relics Protection Units. Besides, Nanfeng Ancient Stove, the oldest wood fired kiln which still in use today, had broken the Guinness World Record.

南风古灶历史照片。
An old photo of Nanfeng Ancient Stove.

遗产名称 / 位置：南风古灶 / 广东省佛山市
Heritage item/Location: Nanfeng Ancient Stove/Foshan City, Guangdong Province

　　南风古灶和高灶生产的器皿在清朝和民国期间已远销南洋，成为佛山"海上丝绸之路"的重要组成部分，被誉为"活态文物"。它们所代表的明代龙窑，是岭南陶瓷产业鼎盛时期的先进生产设备代表，更是石湾陶瓷生产技术进步的里程碑。20世纪80年代，石湾也成为中国现代建筑陶瓷工业化的起点，成为改革开放之后全国产量最大、技术最先进的陶瓷产业基地；两条龙窑可谓"点燃了中国现代建陶工业的第一把火"。因此，南风古灶和高灶具有很高的历史价值、科学价值、社会价值和艺术价值。

　　The pottery produced by Nanfeng Ancient Stove and High Stove were sold far to Nanyang during Qing Dynasty and Republic of China, becoming an important part of Foshan's "Maritime Silk Road", and was praised as "living cultural relic". These Ming dragon kilns represented the advanced production equipments in the heyday of the Lingnan ceramics industry and was the milestone of Shiwan ceramic production technology progress. In the 1980s, Shiwan also became the starting point of industrialization of modern building ceramics industry in China, and the ceramic industrial base with the largest output and the most advanced technology after the reform and opening up. It can be said that the two kilns lit up China's modern ceramic industry. Therefore, Nanfeng Ancient Stove and High Stove are of high historical value, scientific value, social value and artistic value.

贰：核心物项
Section two: Core items

　　南风灶和高灶石湾龙窑主体构筑（包括地基、窑炉炉头、窑室、窑尾、窑棚）。
　　Main construction of Nanfeng Ancient Stove and High Stove of Shiwan dragon kins (including foundation, kiln head, kiln room, kiln tail and kiln shed).

龙窑窑头、窑背。
The head and back of the dragon kiln.

龙窑窑尾。
Dragon kiln tail.

广东

国家工业遗产（第三批）

龙窑出窑的艺术品。
Works of art made from dragon kiln.

龙窑窑门。
Gate of dragon kiln.

龙窑窑背火眼：南风古灶全长 34.4 米，窑背上有 29 排火眼。
A fire hole on the back of the dragon kiln: Nanfeng Ancient Stove is 34.4 meters long and has 29 rows of fire holes on the back of the kiln.

龙窑窑膛内部。
Inside of dragon kiln.

国家工业遗产（第三批）

叁：遗产活化
Section three: Revitalization

南风古灶内的陶笛乐坊。
Ocarina music house in Nanfeng Ancient Stove.

遗产名称/位置：南风古灶 / 广东省佛山市
Heritage item/Location: Nanfeng Ancient Stove/Foshan City, Guangdong Province

广东

南风古灶和高灶两条龙窑现状全景。
Panoramic view of Nanfeng Ancient Stove and High Stove.

国家工业遗产（第三批）

核工业816工程

乌江之畔的世界人工奇迹
Man Made Wonders of the World on the Banks of Wujiang River

壹：遗产春秋
Section one: History

1966年9月10日，中央批准建设"816地下核工程"。该工程位于重庆市涪陵区的乌江之畔、金子山下，占地面积为10.4万平方米。816地下核工程建设期间，经历了急建、缓建、停建3个阶段，先后投入6万多名建设大军，打山洞用时8年、安装设备用时9年。

In September 10th, 1966, Central Government approved the "Underground Nuclear Project 816" alongside the Wujiang River at the foot of Jinzi Mountain in Fuling district of Chongqing. Covering an area of 104 thousand square meters, the project undergone three phrases: high speed, low pace, suspension. Its construction workers amounted to over 60 thousand, who spent 8 years digging burrows and 9 years installing the equipment.

816地下核工程各种支洞相连，有20余千米长。主洞室高达79.6米，拱顶跨高31.2米，完全隐藏在山体内部。洞内共有大型洞室18个，道路、导洞、支洞、隧道及竖井130多条，洞内楼层功能分布明显，宛如迷宫，具有独特的结构之美。816地下核工程的设计和建设代表了当时我国建筑设计、工程建设的最高水平，曾获得国家科技大会奖集体奖。

Underground Nuclear Project 816, with multiple interlinked branch burrows, lasts over 20 kilometers. Its main burrow, completely hidden inside the mountain, reaches as high as 79.6 meters, and its vault 31.2 meters. Inside there are 18 large holes, and over 130 roads, guide holes, branches, tunnels and shafts. Each hole is like a maze, with floors varying with functions, presenting a unique structure of aesthetic value. The design and construction of Underground Nuclear Project 816 represented the highest level of architectural design and engineering construction in China at that time, and won the group award of the National Science and Technology Congress.

816地下核工程建设场景。
Construction sight of Underground Nuclear Project 816.

遗产名称/位置：核工业816工程/重庆市
Heritage item/Location: Nuclear Industry—Project 816/ Chongqing City

2002年4月，国防科工委下发科工密办〔2002〕14号文件，同意对816地下核工程解密。2010年4月，816地下核工程以旅游产品的形式对游客开放，吸引了来自全国各地众多游客前来参观。

In April 2002, the Commission of Science, Technology and Industry for National Defense issued document No.14 of the Office of Science and Technology (2002) approving of the opening-up of Underground Nuclear Project 816. In April 2010, Underground Nuclear Project 816 was opened to tourists, attracting many visitors from all over the country.

贰：核心物项
Section two: Core items

堆工机械加工厂，配套取水制水装置，配套职工生活区，烈士陵园；历史档案。
Heap machinery processing plant, water in-taking equipment, workers' neighborhood, martyrs' mausoleum; historical archives.

烈士陵园（重庆市市级文物）。工程兵五十四师因修建816地下核工程牺牲的76名解放军官兵埋骨于"一碗水"烈士陵园，平均年龄21岁，见证着816地下核工程艰苦卓绝的历程。
Martyrs' mausoleum (Chongqing Municipal Cultural Relics). The 76 PLA officers and soldiers who had died in the construction of Underground Nuclear Project 816 were buried in the "one bowl of water" Martyrs' Mausoleum. Their average age were only 21 years old. The mausoleum witnessed the arduous course of Underground Nuclear Project 816.

816地下核工程配套取水制水装置。20世纪70年代建成投用的供水系统，是白涛地区唯一的取水、供水设施，停军转民后实施了取水口泵房改造和水厂改造，现主要提供生产和生活用水。
Water in-taking equipment of Underground Nuclear Project 816. The water in-taking equipment was ompleted in the 1970s. As the only water in-taking, water supply spot in Baitao area, it was turned into pumping room for in-taking water and water plant after military-to-civilian service transformation. Now it mainly provides water for production and livelihood.

重庆

堆工机械加工厂。原为816地下核工程洞体工程配套提供堆工机械设备安装和维修服务的机械加工中心，随着企业产业结构调整，2009年正式停用。2018年8月，重庆建峰工业集团有限公司与重庆百仓文化创意有限公司合建816核军工小镇文化创意园，打造集军工文化体验、军工设备展陈，以及餐饮娱乐、乡村休闲旅游为一体的综合体。

Heap machinery processing plant. Originally it was the machinery processing center providing equipment installation and maintenance services for burrows of Underground Nuclear Project 816. Following the policy of industrial restructure, it was officially closed in 2009. In August 2018, Chongqing Jianfeng Industrial Group Co., Ltd. and Chongqing Baicang Culture and Creative Co., Ltd. jointly built Cultural and Creative Park of Nuclear Military Industrial Town 816. There tourists can enjoy military-industrial culture, military equipments exhibition, catering and entertainment, and rural recreation.

816地下核工程配套职工生活区。1966年开始与816地下核工程同期建设，有学校、医院等完整的生活配套设施，目前还保存有大量具有三线特色的各类办公场所和居民楼50余栋，如机关大楼、消防岗楼、食堂、露天电影场等。

Workers' neighborhood of Underground Nuclear Project 816. The neighborhood started construction in 1966, the same time when Underground Nuclear Project 816 began construction. In worker's neighborhood, there were such living facilities as schools and hospitals. Now there are still over 50 various of office and residential buildings with Three-Front characteristics, such as the office building, fire fighting building canteen and open-air movie theater.

遗产名称 / 位置：核工业 816 工程 / 重庆市
Heritage item/Location: Nuclear Industry—Project 816/ Chongqing City

叁：遗产活化
Section three: Revitalization

816 小镇介绍
The Introduction of 816 Town

816 小镇由重庆建峰工业集团有限公司提供工业遗址厂房及设备，由具有丰富城市更新、乡村振兴经验的重庆北仓集团投资、改造及运营。

816 industrial site factory and equipment are provided by Chongqing Jianfeng Industrial Group Co., Ltd., invested, renovated and operated by Chongqing Beicang Group, which has rich experience in urban renewal and rural revitalization.

重庆

816 军工陈列馆。816 Military Exhibition Hall.

堆工机械加工厂仓库改造成的"星光书院"。
"Xingguang Academy" transformed from warehouse of heap machinery processing plant.

816 小镇内的印证历史过往的山楂树。
Hawthorn trees in 816 town witness to the past.

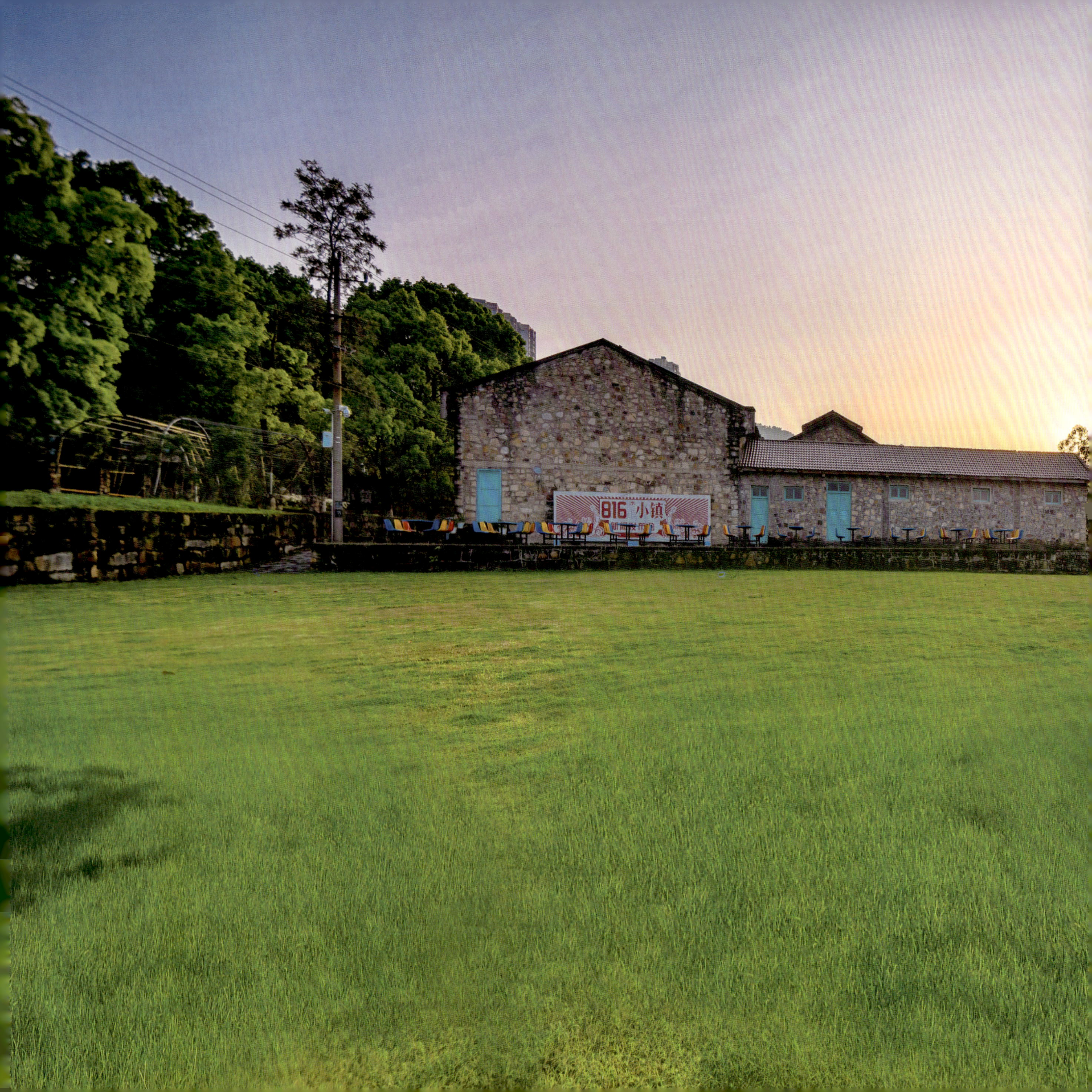
816 小镇

816 小镇。Town 816.

国家工业遗产（第三批）

重庆长风化工厂

中国特种光气衍生物重要生产基地
An Important Production Base of Special Phosgene Derivatives

壹：遗产春秋
Section one: History

　　军工配套企业重庆长风化工厂，始建于20世纪60年代"三线建设"时期，拥有研发和生产用于军事的专用化学品的专门技术体系和能力，是中国特种光气衍生物的重要生产基地和部分军用化学品惟一定点生产企业，在光气职业病防治、光气中毒研究及临床治疗等方面处于全国领先水平。其建成和投产，扭转了西南国防工业配套产品依赖外区供应的被动局面。

　　Founded in the 1960s during the Third-Front movement, Chongqing Changfeng Chemical Plant, a military supporting enterprise, was able to develop and produce special chemicals for military use. It is an important production base of special phosgene derivatives and the only designated manufacturer of some military chemicals in China, leading the research on phosgene occupational disease prevention, phosgene poisoning and clinical treatment. Because of the plant, the supply of supporting products for the southwest defense industry no longer depends on other regions.

原厂区全貌。
Panoramic view of the original plant.

遗产名称/位置：重庆长风化工厂/重庆市长寿区
Heritage item/Location: Chongqing Changfeng Chemical Plant/Changshou District,Chongqing City

贰：核心物项
Section two: Core items

光气合成生产线，中定剂生产线，工人俱乐部，单身宿舍及职工食堂，生活水塔；历史档案。
Phosgenesynthesis production line, intermediates production line, Workers'club, single dormitory and staff canteen, living water tower; historical archives.

原厂区大门。
Gate of the original plant.

原职工食堂。
The original staff canteen.

浮阀塔。
Float valve tower.

重庆

国家工业遗产（第三批）

工人俱乐部原貌。
The original Workers' club.

光气合成生产线。
Phosgenesynthesis production line.

生活水塔。
Living water tower.

遗产名称 / 位置：重庆长风化工厂 / 重庆市长寿区
Heritage item/Location: Chongqing Changfeng Chemical Plant/Changshou District,Chongqing City

叁：遗产今夕
Section three: Current Situation

　　重庆长风化工厂坐落在西南重镇重庆长寿区东南方向 12 千米的黄桷岩区域。按照国家光气建设生产区环境安全等相关要求，重庆长风化工厂将于 2020 年搬迁。届时，原址区域内的生产装置、厂房等将作为工业遗产被妥善保护。

Chongqing Changfeng Chemical Plant is located in Huangjueyan area, 12 kilometers southeast of Changshou District, Chongqing City, an important city in southwest China. Chongqing Changfeng Chemical Plant will be relocated in 2020 in accordance with the environmental safety requirements of the national phosgene construction and production area. At that time, the production facilities and workshops within the original site will be properly protected as an industrial heritage.

重庆长风化工厂大门。
Gate of Chongqing Changfeng Chemical Plant.

厂区现状全景。
Panoramic view of the current plant.

重庆

国家工业遗产（第三批）

成都水井街酒坊

浓香型白酒酿造工艺实物史书
A Physical History of Strong Aromatic Spirits Brewing Craftwork

壹：遗产春秋
Section one: History

　　成都水井街酒坊始建于元末明初，延续600余年从未间断生产。成都水井街酒坊遗址揭示了中国浓香型白酒酿造的全过程，是白酒制造工业领域珍贵的实物资料。水井坊酒传统酿造技艺2008年6月被国务院列为国家级非物质文化遗产。

　　Chengdu Shuijing Street Distillery was founded in the late Yuan and early Ming Dynasties, and has been in continuous production for more than 600 years. The site of Chengdu Shuijing Street Distillery reveals the whole brewing process of strong aromatic Chinese spirits and serves as a precious material in the field of liquor manufacturing industry. The whole flow of the traditional spirits brewing craftwork was listed as a National Intangible Cultural Heritage by the State Council in June 2008.

　　成都水井街酒坊遗址面积约1 700平方米，发掘面积280平方米。遗迹包括晾堂3座、酒窖8口、灶坑4座、灰坑4个、灰沟1条、蒸馏设备冷凝器基座、路基、石条墙基、木柱及柱础等。出土文物以陶瓷酒具、食具为主。遗址完整复原了浓香型白酒的酿造全过程，被白酒专家、考古专家誉为中国白酒行业的"兵马俑""中国浓香型白酒酿造工艺的一部无字史书"，为研究中国蒸馏酒酿造工艺的发展历程提供了珍贵的第一手材料，丰富了中国传统酒文化的研究内容。

　　The total area of this site is more than 1 700 square meters, with altogether 280 square meters of which has been excavated. The relics include three air-curing terraces, eight bodegas, four cooking pits, four ash pits, one ash ditch, condenser base of distillation equipment, roadbed, stone strip wall foundation, wooden column and column base. Food and beverage utensils were mainly unearthed from the site. The whole brewing process of strong aromatic Chinese spirits is reproduced in the site, which is praised as "the Terracotta Army" of China's liquor industry and "a history book without words on the brewing craftwork of strong aromatic liquor in China" by liquor experts and archaeologists. It provides valuable first-hand materials for studying the development of Chinese distilled wine brewing technology and enriches Chinese traditional wine culture.

遗产名称/位置：成都水井街酒坊/四川省成都市
Heritage item/Location: Chengdu Shuijing Street Distillery/Chengdu City, Sichuan Province

四川

成都水井街酒坊遗产项目的所在地成都老东门，曾是商贾云集、店铺和作坊鳞次栉比的繁华市井，图为用沙盘再现的东门胜景。
The old east gate of Chengdu, where the heritage project of Chengdu Shuijing Street distillery is located, was once a bustling market with merchants, shops and workshops. The picture shows the beautiful scenery of the East Gate reappeared with sand table.

国家工业遗产（第三批）

贰：核心物项
Section two: Core items

"T"字型结构制酒生产车间，L1-L3晾堂，J1-J8窖池，老1-老22窖池，新1-新40窖池，Z1-Z4灶坑，蒸馏设备冷凝器基座，路基，散水，柱础。

T-shaped structure wine production workshop, L1-L3 air-curing terraces, J1-J8 liquor pits, old 1- old 22 liquor pits, new 1- new 40 liquor pits, Z1-Z4 cooking pits, condenser base of distillation equipment, roadbed, apron, column base.

明代窖池发掘现场。
Excavation site of liquor pits in Ming Dynasty.

全国重点文物保护单位——成都水井街酒坊遗址。
The ruins of Chengdu Shui Jing Jie Jiu Fang, a National Key Cultural Relic Protection Unit.

遗产名称 / 位置：成都水井街酒坊 / 四川省成都市
Heritage item/Location: Chengdu Shuijing Street Distillery/Chengdu City, Sichuan Province

叁：遗产活化
Section three: Revitalization

成都水井街酒坊现今仍在使用。水井街酒坊遗址属于土遗址，出现了部分开裂、酥碱等土质文物特有的病害现象，但因处于博物馆的室内环境中，保存较为完整。

Chengdu Shuijingjie Jiufang Heritage Project is still in use today. The site of Shuijingjie Jiufang belongs to earthen ruins, which has some special diseases of earthen relics, such as partial cracking, Crisp Alkali, etc..

四川

复原的明代街景。
A restored streetscape of Ming Dynasty.

国家工业遗产（第三批）

  2013年成立的以工业遗产及传统酒文化为展示主题的水井坊博物馆，原址原貌地保存了成都水井街酒坊的现状，并以真实的生产场景再现600余年历史的水井坊酒传统酿造技艺，是水井坊酒国家原产地域保护的地标中心和主要生产场所之一，更是将实际生产过程和展示陈列完美融为一体的"活"的博物馆。

  Established in 2013, the Shuijingfang Museum takes industrial heritage and traditional wine culture as its theme, which recreates exactly the production scene of Chengdu Shuijing Street Distillery and demonstrates traditional brewing techniques inherited for more than 600 years. As a landmark center for the national original area protection of Shuijingfang Wine and one of the main production site , this "living" museum integrates the actual production process and display perfectly.

展示国家级非物质文化遗产——水井坊酒传统酿造技艺的现场生产区。
An on site production area showcasing the traditional brewing techniques of Intangible Cultural Heritage.

遗产名称/位置：成都水井街酒坊/四川省成都市
Heritage item/Location: Chengdu Shuijing Street Distillery/Chengdu City, Sichuan Province

四川

现场生产和接酒。
Liquor production and relaying on site.

国家工业遗产（第三批）

自贡井盐

千年盐都的手作史记
A Millennium History of Hand-mining Well Salt

壹：遗产春秋
Section one: History

自贡地区的井盐生产发端于2 000年前的东汉时期。在东汉时期和南北朝时期就分别出现了以富世井、大公井为代表的盐井，在明清时期迅速发展。新中国成立之后，自贡盐业生产逐步发展成为独立的行业，成为了盐化工基地。1978年后，自贡盐业进入稳定、持续发展的新时期。

Well salt production in Zigong began in the Eastern Han Dynasty about 2 000 years ago. In the Eastern Han Dynasty and the Southern and Northern Dynasties, salt wells, represented by Fushi Well and Dagong Well, developed rapidly in the Ming and Qing Dynasties. After the founding of the people's Republic of China, Zigong salt industry gradually developed into an independent industry and a salt chemical base. After 1978, Zigong salt industry entered a new period of stable and sustainable development.

自贡井盐大安盐场鸟瞰图。
Aerial view of Da'an Salt Plant of Zigong Well Salt.

遗产名称/位置：自贡井盐/四川省自贡市
Heritage item/Location: Zigong Well Salt/ Zigong City, Sichuan Province

东源井天车。Dongyuanjing crane.

　　如今，随着盐业生产的现代化，机械采盐早已彻底取代了手工采盐。盐都大地上曾经密如森林的井架和天车也逐渐淡出人们的视野。回望千年盐都的历史，井盐的兴衰始终贯穿其中：始建于1957年的大安盐厂，曾是自贡市最大的盐厂；世界第一口超千米深井燊海井至今仍然保留着千年的传统手工制盐，已成为我国土法生产井盐的活化石；在一百多年的采矿制盐过程中，从未间断生产的东源井至今依然高产。

　　Today, with the modernization of salt production, mechanical salt mining has already completely replaced manual salt mining. The derrick and crown block that used to be dense as forest on the land of Salt Copital gradually faded out of people's view. Looking back on the history of the Salt Capital for thousands of years, the rise and fall of well salt always run through it: it was built in 1957 Da'an Salt Plant was once the largest salt plant in Zigong City, and the Shenhai Well, the world's first well with a depth of more than 1 000 meters, still retains the traditional manual salt production for thousands of years, and has become a living fossil of well salt production by indigenous method in China. In the process of mining and salt production for more than 100 years, Dongyuan Well, which has never been interrupted, is still high-yield.

　　自贡制盐工艺的历史与发展，见证了千年盐都的辉煌与工业文化遗产的悠久魅力，已成为我国手工采盐业的历史见证。

　　The history and development of the Zigong salt-making process have witnessed the glory of the thousand-year-old Salt Capital and the age-old glamour of the industrial cultural heritage, exhibiting China's hand-mining salt industry.

四川

贰：核心物项
Section two: Core items

　　大安盐厂：真空制盐主厂房及真空制盐设备，热水池，储物仓库，软水房，59号盐仓，白水泵房，水塔，波钢塔，输盐传输带通道，沉淀池。

　　Da'an Salt Plant: vacuum salt-making plant and vacuum salt-making equipments, hot water pool, warehouse, soft water room, No.59 salt warehouse, clear water pump room, water tower, wave steel tower, salt conveyor belt, precipitation pool.

整改前的大安盐场全景。
Panorama of Da'an Salt Plant before revamping.

遗产名称 / 位置：自贡井盐 / 四川省自贡市
Heritage item/Location: Zigong Well Salt/ Zigong City, Sichuan Province

东源井：矿井，木制井架，井帽子，篾盆，烟巷，碓房，过浆房，机车房，大车房，小车房，平锅制盐作坊，踩架；地辊，天辊，机车，木质大车，马槽辊子，大木楻桶，车心石，输气沟道。

Dongyuan Well: mine, wooden head-frame, well cover, Kang basin, smoke alley, heap room, syrup room, locomotive room, large garage, small garage, pan salt-making workshop, treading frame; floor roller, sky roller, locomotive, wooden cart, manger roller, large wooden barrel, Chexin stone gas pipeline.

东源井古盐场。
Old salt plant of Dongyuan Well.

平锅制盐场景。
Pan salt-making scene.

东源井烟巷。
Smoke alley of Dongyuan Well.

燊海井：碓房及打井设备和井口，大车房及卷扬机房，灶房及制盐设施设备，柜房，盐仓；天车，大车，笕管，楻桶，烟巷，晒卤台。

Shenhai Well: heap room and well drilling equipments and wellhead, large garage and rolling-up machine room, stove room and salt-making facilities and equipments, cabinet room, salt warehouse; overhead crane, large cart, halogen pipe, bucket, smoke alley, halogen drying platform.

晒卤台。
Halogen drying platform.

灶房。
Stove room.

楻桶。
Bucket.

四川

203

叁：遗产活化
Section three: Revitalization

　　昔日自贡市的最大盐厂——大安盐厂，如今变身为老盐场1957项目园区，建成盐知道文创店、迷你盐博馆、荣宝斋画展厅、书屋等工业文化项目，成为当地的文化地标。

　　Da'an Salt Plant, once the largest salt plant in Zigong City, has now been transformed into old salt plant 1957 project park, and has become a local cultural landmark by establishing industrial and cultural projects such as Salt Common Sense cultural and creative gift shop, Mini Salt Museum, Rongbaozhai Painting Exhibition Hall and book house.

　　东源井目前已完成传统工艺制盐展示馆。

　　Dongyuan Well has now completed the exhibition hall for traditional salt-making craft.

　　燊海井自1988年成为全国重点文物保护单位以来，已建设成为全国性的科普和爱国主义教育基地、自贡世界地质公园重要组成部分，成为自贡市对外接待的重要旅游窗口。2018年，燊海井景区接待游客约13万人。2001年—2019年3月，燊海井景区通过展示工业遗址实现旅游门票和旅游商品收入1 922万元，在实现经济与社会效益双赢的同时，让自贡井盐传统的熬制和深钻技艺在历史长河中长存不衰。

　　Since enlisted into a key cultural relic protection unit nationwide in 1988, Shenhai Well has become a national education base for science and patriotism, an important part of Zigong World Geo-park, and an important tourism ground for receiving outsiders. In 2018, its scenic area received about 130 000 visitors. From 2001 to March 2019, Shenhai Well tourist spot made a revenue of 19.22 million yuan through selling tickets and souvenirs. The display of industrial sites brings a win-win economic and social result, so that the traditional production method and deep drilling skills of Zigong Well Salt pass on through the long history.

即将布局为自贡市文创实践基地的59号盐仓。
No. 59 salt warehouse will be set up as Zigong cultural and creative practice base.

真空制盐法生产出盐后，将通过传送带运送到盐仓。目前，大安盐场输盐传输带通道已打造成为艺术画廊。
Salt made by vacuum workshop will be transported to salt warehouse via a conveyor belt. At present, salt conveyor belt of Da'an Salt Plant has been built into an art gallery.

遗产名称/位置：自贡井盐/四川省自贡市
Heritage item/Location: Zigong Well Salt/ Zigong City, Sichuan Province

四川

海井活化利用展示。
Display of Shenhai well activation and utilization.

205

国家工业遗产（第三批）

攀枝花钢铁厂

中国钢铁工业的骄傲
The Pride of China's Iron and Steel Industry

壹：遗产春秋
Section one: History

攀枝花钢铁厂（以下简称"攀钢"）始建于1965年，1970年建成投产，是我国第一家完全依靠自己的力量建设起来的我国战略后方最大的钢铁工业基地，1号高炉、提钒炼钢厂1号转炉等设备都是由我国自行设计、制造的首台(套)产品，被誉为"中国钢铁工业的骄傲"。攀钢是我国"三线建设"的具体承载和典型代表，结束了我国西部没有大型钢铁企业的历史。目前，遗产群主体部分仍在生产使用。

Founded in 1965 and put into production in 1970, Panzhihua Iron and Steel Works (Panzhihua Steel), fully relied on its own strength to build up, is the first and largest steelmaker in the strategic rear of China. Many equipments designed and manufactured by China itself, such as No.1 blast furnace and No.1 converter in vanadium extraction steel plant, are the first (set) products in China. It is a typical representative of the Third-Front movement in China, praised as "the pride of China's iron and steel industry", ending the history of no large-scale iron and steel enterprises in Western China. At present, the main part of the heritage group is still in production.

攀钢1号高炉于1970年7月1日点火开炉，高炉容积1 000立方米，是新中国成立后完全由我国自行设计的高炉，结束了我国西部没有大型钢铁企业的历史。
Pangzhihua Steel No.1 blast furnace was put into production on July 1st, 1970, with a capacity of 1 000 cubic meters. No.1 blast furnace was designed by China itself after the founding of China, ending the history of no large-scale iron and steel enterprises in Western China.

遗产名称/位置：攀枝花钢铁厂/四川省攀枝花市
Heritage item/Location: Panzhihua Iron and Steel Works/Panzhihua City, Sichuan Province

贰：核心物项
Section two: Core items

朱家包包铁矿（含狮子山大爆破遗址），弄弄坪主厂区工业建筑群，兰家火山大坪硐，渡口造船厂船坞及码头；攀钢1号高炉，提钒炼钢厂1号转炉，3#汽轮鼓风机组，009#电力机车。

Zhujia Baobao Iron Mine (including the major blasting site of Lion Mountain), the industrial complex of Nongnongping Main Factory, Lanjia Volcano Great Adit, dock and wharf of Dukou Shipyard, Pangzhihua Steel No.1 blast furnace, No.1 converter in vanadium extraction steel plant, 3# turbo-blower group, 009# electric locomotive.

兰家火山大坪硐于1966年开始建设，建设过程中实现了月成硐300米，创造了全国铁路隧道掘进成硐最新记录，1966年7月，郭沫若视察平硐建设并书写了"兰家火山大平硐"七个大字，被雕刻在平硐上方。

The construction of Lanjia Volcano Great Adit began in 1966, with 300 meters of cave completed every month, setting a new record for railway tunneling construction speed in China. In July 1966, Guo Moruo inspected the construction of the adit and wrote seven Chinese characters, "Lanjia Volcano Great Adit", which are carved above the adit.

国家工业遗产（第三批）

009#电力机车于1970年11月投入使用，型号G150-1500-1，自重150吨，是攀钢主要铁路运输设备，2015年停用，代表了当时铁路运输设备制造的国内先进水平。
009# electric locomotive was put into use in November 1970. The model G150-1500-1, with a dead weight of 150 tons, is the main railway transportation equipment of Panzhihua Steel, which represents the domestic advanced level of railway transportation equipment manufacturing at that time. It was discontinued in 2015.

作为攀钢一期建设配套工程，3#汽轮鼓风机组于1975年投产，额定功率12MW，是由我国自行设计制造的风机。
As a supporting project for the first phase construction of Panzhihua Steel, 3# turbo-blower group was put into production in 1975 with rated power of 12MW. It was designed and manufactured by China itself.

提钒炼钢厂1号转炉于1971年10月1日建成投产，是我国第一座自行设计、制造、建设的120吨级大型转炉，是攀钢一期工程建设的核心项目之一。

No.1 converter in vanadium extraction steel plant was put into operation on October 1st, 1971 and was the first large-scale converter of 120-ton designed and manufactured by China itself. It is one of the core projects of first phase construction of Panzhihua Steel.

叁：遗产今夕
Section three: Current Situation

近年来，攀钢及时启动工业遗产保护工作，对仍在生产使用的工业遗产，加强日常维护，确保本体安全。同时，积极推动产线形象展示，打造生产区域精品参观路线，拓宽社会公众走近工业遗产的途径，实现工业遗产的科学开发与再利用。

In recent years, Pangzhihua Steel started the protection of industrial heritage in time. To preserve the heritage, it strengthened the daily maintenance of industrial heritage which is still in production and use. At the same time, in order to actively promote the image display of the production line, it created excellent visiting routes in the production area, broadening the way for the public to approach the industrial heritage, and realizing the scientific development and reuse of the industrial heritage.

狮子山原貌。
Original appeareance of Lion Mountain.

狮子山现貌。Current view of Lion Mountain.

遗产名称/位置：攀枝花钢铁厂/四川省攀枝花市
Heritage item/Location: Panzhihua Iron and Steel Works/Panzhihua City, Sichuan Province

四川

弄弄坪主厂区工业建筑群于1965年开工建设，打破我国钢铁工业传统的布局方式，在面积仅有2.5平方千米、高差达80米的狭窄山坡上，采取3个大台阶、23个小台阶的竖向布局法，精心设计建设了大型钢铁联合企业，吨钢占地面积仅为0.4平方米，被誉为"象牙微雕钢城"。

The construction of the industrial complex of Nongnongping Main Factory was started in 1965, which broke the traditional layout of China's iron and steel industry. On the narrow hillside with an area of only 2.5 square kilometers and a height difference of 80 meters, 3 large steps and 23 small steps were adopted for the vertical layout of a large iron and steel joint enterprise. With an area of only 0.4 square meters per ton of steel, it is known as "engraved ivory miniature of steel city".

国家工业遗产（第三批）

洞窝水电站

第一座中国人自主设计建设的水电站
The First Hydroelectric Station Designed and Built by Chinese

壹：遗产春秋
Section one: History

中国兵器工业集团有限公司北化研究院集团泸州北方化学工业有限公司洞窝水电站（以下简称"洞窝水电站"）原名济和水力发电厂，始建于1921年，1925年建成发电，是中国人自行设计和施工的第一座水电站，现存三台机组、两座厂房。

North Chemical Research Institute Group Luzhou North Chemical Industry Co., Ltd. Dongwo Hydroelectric Station (Dongwo Hydroelectric Station), formerly known as Jihe Hydroelectricity. Its construction began in 1921; after completion of construction in 1925, it started to generate electricity. It was the first hydroelectric station designed and constructed by Chinese, with three generating units and two plants left.

洞窝水电站外景。Periphery of Dongwo Hydroelectric Station.

遗产名称/位置：洞窝水电站/四川省泸州市
Heritage item/Location: Dongwo Hydroelectric Station/ Luzhou City, Sichuan Province

洞窝水电站体现了我国当时水电工程、设计工程的最高水平。税西恒在龙溪河积极探索梯级开发，形成了一级洞窝坝、二级谷西滩坝、三级特陵桥坝三级堤坝，其后龙溪河建设了五座电站，形成了五个梯级电站群，体现了中国治水用水的传统智慧。梯级开发为我国此后的金沙江、大渡河等梯级开发提供了经验。

Dongwo Hydroelectric Station embodies the highest level of hydroelectric engineering design in China at that time. Shuixiheng actively explored the cascade development of Longxi River, forming a first-class Dongwo dam, a second-class Guxitan dam, and a third-class Telingqiao dam. Subsequently, five power stations were built on Longxi River and five cascade power stations were formed, reflect the traditional wisdom of water control and utilization. Ladder development has provided experience for the utilization of the Jinsha River and the Dadu River in China.

洞窝水电站抗战军工文物见证了中国军工企业的发展历程，体现了浓厚的爱国主义精神，具有重要的政治意义和服务国家与人民的时代意义，是见证中国近代早期水电工程建设发展的代表性遗产。

Anti-Japanese War relics of Dongwo Hydroelectric Station witness the development of China's military enterprises, embody the strong spirit of patriotism, have important political significance and epic significance of serving the country and its people, and are the representative heritage's witnessing the construction and development of hydroelectric projects in the early days of China.

贰：核心物项
Section two: Core items

拦河坝，引水渠，厂房；发电机组；《泸县济和水力发电厂股份有限公司营业工程两部说明表》。
Barrage, diversion canal, factory building, generating set, *Two instructions for the Operation of Luxian JiheHydroelectric Power Plant Co., Ltd.*.

引水渠。Diversion canal.

美国通用发电机组。American general generating set.

四川

税西恒
Shui Xiheng

税西恒，名绍圣，四川省泸州市人，1912年公费赴德留学生，由于成绩优异，获得德国国家工程师称号，在西门子电力公司担任工程师。

Shui Xiheng, alias Shao Sheng, was a native of Luzhou City, Sichuan Province. In 1912, he went to study in Germany at state expense. Because of his excellent performance, he won the title of German National Engineer, and became an engineer at Siemens Electric Power Company.

1921年，税西恒回国立志兴业报国。他注意到西南地区有着丰富的水利资源，十分利于水电开发。经过大量的水文、地理和地质勘测后，税西恒选定了龙溪河最末一个梯级——洞窝，作为水电站的建设地。面对启动资金缺乏的困难，税西恒变卖部分田产，带头认购2 500元股金，保证了施工的顺利推进。1925年，终于建成水力发电厂。

In 1921, Shui Xiheng returned to China to make a contribution to his motherland. He noted that the southwest region was rich in water resources, and thus was suitable for hydroelectric development. After much work done in terms of hydro-logic, geographical and geological surveys, Shui xiheng chose the last cascade of the Longxi River—Dongwo as the construction site of hydroelectric station. To raise funds for construction, Shui xiheng sold part of his landed property and took the lead in buying 2 500 yuan of share to ensure construction. In 1925, the hydroelectric station was completed.

税西恒（1889—1980）
Shui Xiheng (1889—1980)

建设期间，由于建材匮乏，税西恒利用当地丰富的石料，采用中国传统水利工程建造常用的糯米浆拌石灰浆粘合砌条石的施工方式，建起了拦河坝、引水渠、厂房及主机基础。如今，这个"糯米工程"仍然固若金汤。由于成功地将西方大坝工程设计理论与中国传统水工建筑材料、施工工艺有机结合，税西恒被誉为"中国小水电之父"。

During the construction, because of the lack of building materials, Shui Xiheng used local stones as the building material. He adopted traditional Chinese hydraulic engineering construction method—strip stones glued by sticky rice syrup and lime slurry in building barricades, water canals, factory buildings and generating base. Today, the "Sticky Rice Project" is still as solid as iron. Due to his contribution in combining western dam engineering design theory with Chinese hydraulic building materials and construction technology, Shui Xiheng earns the title of "father of China's small hydroelectric".

遗产名称/位置：洞窝水电站/四川省泸州市
Heritage item/Location: Dongwo Hydroelectric Station/ Luzhou City, Sichuan Province

叁：遗产活化
Section three: Revitalization

近百年来，洞窝水电站已累计发电3亿多千瓦时，至今仍承担着为企业供电的功能。

In the past one hundred years, Dongwo Hydroelectric Station has generated more than 300 million kilowatt hours of electricity. Up to now, it still provides electricity for enterprises.

鉴于洞窝水电站的历史价值，又因其位于长江左岸支流龙溪河下游，处于国家3A级景区洞窝景区内，具有独特的峡谷风景，洞窝拦河坝、洞窝断崖瀑布、乳峰奇观等景观险、奇、幽、秀，非常迷人，泸州北方化学工业有限公司十分注重保护利用。目前，洞窝水电站获批第八批全国重点文物保护单位、全国中小学生研学实践基地、第二批九三学社全国传统教育基地，整体遗产文物群年接待量超过10万人次。

Dongwo Hydroelectric Station is located downstream of the Longxi River, tributary on the left bank of the Yangtze River, incorporated into the national 3A-class Dongwo scenic area, it has a unique canyon landscape. Among the adventurous, amazing, secluded, splendid tourists spots are Dongwo barrage, Dongwo cliff waterfall and Ru peak wonders. In view of the historical value and glamour of Dongwo Hydroelectric Station, Luzhou North Chemical Industry Co., Ltd. attaches great importance to its protection and utilization. At present, Dongwo Hydropower Station has obtained the eighth batch of National Key Cultural Relic Protection Units, the national primary and Secondary School Students Nationwide by the Ministry of education, and the second batch of the National Traditional Education base of Jiusan Society. Its cultural relics attracts more than 100 000 people every year.

洞窝风景区。Dongwo landscape.

四川

国家工业遗产（第三批）

洞窝水电站二级堤坝谷西滩坝。
Guxitan dam—second-class dam of Dongwo Hydroelectric Station.

洞窝水电站三级堤坝特陵桥坝。
Telingqiao dam—third-class dam of Dongwo Hydroelectric Station.

参考资料：《税西恒传》。Reference: *Biography of Shui Xiheng*.

拦河坝。
Barrage.

隆昌气矿圣灯山气田旧址

中国天然气工业摇篮和天然气槽法炭黑起源地
The Cradle of China's Natural Gas Industry and the Origin of Carbon Black in Natural Gas Tank

壹：遗产春秋
Section one: History

　　圣灯山气田自古便有浅层天然气溢出燃烧。隆昌气矿圣灯山气田旧址原为石油工业部四川石油勘探局（四川石油管理局前身）隆昌气矿的矿区和隆昌炭黑厂的厂区。圣灯山气田于1943年开钻隆2井，1951年国家利用该井所产天然气试制出我国第一批天然气槽法炭黑，打破西方封锁，发展了祖国橡胶工业。1955年圣灯山气田上诞生了我国最早的现代天然气建制工业气矿——隆昌气矿。

Shallow gas overflows and Burns in Shengdeng Mountain Gas Field since ancient times. The site of Shengdeng Mountain Gas Field in Longchang Gas Mine was originally the mine area of Longchang Gas Mine and the plant area of Longchang Carbon Black Plant of Sichuan Petroleum Exploration Bureau (the predecessor of Sichuan Petroleum Administration Bureau) . In 1943, No.2 Long Well was drilled in Shengdeng Mountain Gas Field, and in 1951, the first batch of natural gas tank carbon black was produced by using the natural gas produced in the well, which broke the Western blockade and developed the rubber industry of our country. In 1955, Shengdeng Mountain Gas Field gave birth to the earliest modern industrial gas deposit in China —— The Longchang Gas Mine.

　　隆昌气矿圣灯山气田旧址作为毛泽东主席生平唯一视察过的石油企业所在地，承载着国民经济三年恢复时期和"一五"计划期间我国天然气工业建设的历史贡献和记忆，在天然气钻探采输、井下作业、制炭黑、脱硫等领域，为中国天然气工业的起步发展奠定了基石，被誉为"中国天然气工业摇篮""中国天然气槽法炭黑起源地""油气红色圣地"。

The site of Shengdeng Mountain Gas Field in Longchang gas mine, as the only site of petroleum enterprise visited by Chairman Mao Zedong, bears the contribution and memory of the construction of China's natural gas industry during three year recovery period of national economy and the first five year plan period. It has laid the foundation for the development of China's natural gas industry in the fields of natural gas drilling, production and transportation, underground operation, carbon black production, desulfurization and so on. Known as "China's natural gas industry cradle" "China's natural gas trough carbon black origin" "oil and gas red holy land".

遗产名称 / 位置：隆昌气矿圣灯山气田旧址 / 四川省内江市隆昌市
Heritage item/Location: Former site of Shengdeng Mountain Gas Field in Longchang Gas Mine/Longchang City, Neijiang City, Sichuan Province.

四川

1958年3月27日毛主席视察隆昌气矿时稍作休息的招待所。
The guest house where Chairman Mao took a rest while inspecting Longchang Gas Mine on March 27th, 1958.

219

贰：核心物项
Section two: Core items

隆2井，隆10井，炭黑车间办公室，炭黑火房遗址，炭黑试验室，隆昌气矿1、2、3号办公楼，传动车间和工人休息室，跃进礼堂，隆昌气矿招待所；20世纪50年代炭黑产品2瓶，炭黑车间回收的硫磺2瓶，炭黑火房的基脚石1块，火嘴1套；《隆昌圣灯山气田地质研究报告（1964年12月）》、天然气槽法炭黑生产工艺设计图纸等历史档案。

No.2 Long Well, No.10 Long Well, carbon black workshop office, carbon black fire house site, carbon black laboratory, No. 1, 2, 3 office building of Longchang Gas Mine, transmission workshop and workers' lounge, Yuejin hall, Longchang Gas Hostel; 2 bottles of carbon black products in the 1950s, 2 bottles of sulfur recovered from the carbon black workshop, 1 base stone of the carbon black fire house, 1 set of fire nozzle, *Geological Research Report of Shengdeng Mountain Gas Field in Longchang (December 1964)*, production process design drawings of carbon black by natural gas tank method and other historical files.

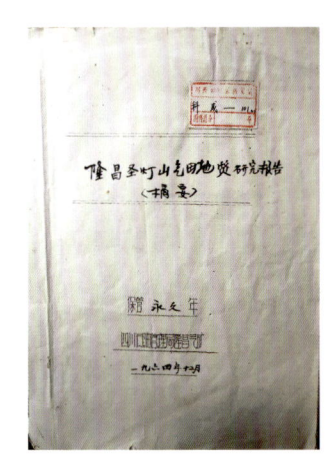

《隆昌圣灯山气田地质研究报告》，首次运用曲率方法表示裂缝发育度，于1964年年底完成。

Geological Research Report of Shengdeng Mountain Gas Field in Longchang used curvature method to express fracture development degree for the first time. The report was completed at the end of 1964.

隆2井，1944年完成井口产气装置，日产气约3.6万立方米，时称"远东第一井"。

No.2 Long Well, was known as "the first well in the Far East". The wellhead gas production device was completed in 1944, with a daily gas output of about 36 000 cubic meters.

隆10井，1955年开钻，四川盆地第一口以二叠系为目的层的预探专层井。

No.10 Long Well was drilled in 1955. It is the first pre-exploration zone well in Sichuan Basin with Permian as the target bed.

遗产名称/位置：隆昌气矿圣灯山气田旧址/四川省内江市隆昌市
Heritage item/Location: Former site of Shengdeng Mountain Gas Field in Longchang Gas Mine/Longchang City, Neijiang City, Sichuan Province.

2号办公楼原貌。
The former view of No.2 office building.

2号办公楼现状。
The current situation of No.2 office building.

四川

建于20世纪50年代的传动车间旧址。
The former site of transmission workshop built in the 1950s.

张铁生：中国炭黑工业奠基人
Zhang Tiesheng: Founder of China's Black Carbon Industry

张铁生，1947年获伊利诺斯大学硕士学位，谢绝挽留归国；1949年愤然离开南京国民政府中央工业试验所；1950年主持筹建隆昌炭黑厂，自主设计、成功试制出我国第一代天然气槽法炭黑。1958—1986年筹建发展四川天然气研究室（所）。在他的领导下，天然气研究利用领域不断拓宽，完成了国家下达的多项重大课题。

Zhang Tiesheng, who received a master degree from the University of Illinois in 1947, declined to stay in foreign country and return to China; In 1949, he left the Central Industrial Laboratory of the Nationalist Government in Nanjing; In 1950, he presided over the construction of Longchang Carbon Black Plant and designed and successfully trial-produced the first generation of natural gas tank carbon black in China. From 1958 to 1986, Sichuan Natural Gas Research Institute was established. Under his leadership, the field of natural gas research and utilization has been broadened, and a number of major projects have been completed.

遗产名称/位置：隆昌气矿圣灯山气田旧址/四川省内江市隆昌市
Heritage item/Location: Former site of Shengdeng Mountain Gas Field in Longchang Gas Mine/Longchang City, Neijiang City, Sichuan Province.

叁：遗产活化
Section three: Revitalization

在20世纪80年代隆昌炭黑厂停产、2014年圣灯山气田停产后，隆昌气矿区域逐渐成为工业文化遗迹，归中国石油西南油气田公司所有。2018年，公司在1996年落成的"毛泽东主席视察隆昌气矿纪念馆"的基础上改造升级，建成总占地11 831平方米、展示区域2 200余平方米的教育基地，包括纪念馆展厅、纪念碑、炭黑火房、炭黑车间建筑旧址等，呈现了新中国成立初期圣灯山气田开发建设、我国第一批天然气槽法炭黑诞生、毛泽东主席视察隆昌气矿炭黑车间等光荣历史，以及四川油气工业发展壮大的光辉历程，现为四川省爱国主义教育基地、四川省国防教育基地、中国石油天然气集团有限公司石油精神教育基地。

Longchang Carbon Black Plant stopped Production in the 1980s, and Shengdeng Mountain Gas Field was closed in 2014, There after, Longchang Gas Field has gradually become an industrial cultural heritage, owned by Petro China Southwest Oil and Gasfield Company. In 2018, based on the "Memorial Hall of Chairman Mao Zedong's Inspection of Longchang Gas Mine" which was completed in 1996, the company built an education base with a total area of 11 831 square meters and a display area of more than 2 200 square meters, including the memorial hall exhibition hall, monument, carbon black fire house, carbon black workshop building site, etc., presenting the construction of Shengdeng Mountain Gas Field in the early days of the People's Republic of China, the first batch of natural gas tank carbon black in China, Chairman Mao Zedong's inspection of the carbon black workshop of Longchang Gas Mine and the glorious course of the development and growth of Sichuan oil and gas industry. Now it is the base of patriotism education in Sichuan Province, the base of national defense education in Sichuan Province, and the base of Petroleum Spirit Education in CNPC.

2018年采取"修旧如旧"方式还原的炭黑火房，分别是：毛泽东主席蹲下视察的21号火房和青年突击队员修建的"跃进号"火房。
The restored black carbon fire houses in the way of "repairing the old as the old" in 2018, namely, No.21 fire house where Chairman Mao Zedong squatted down for inspection and "Yuejin" fire house.

纪念馆展厅通过图文、视频及珍贵藏品，展呈了在党和国家领导人的亲切关怀下，四川省油气工业从无到有、发展壮大的光荣历程和难忘瞬间。
The exhibition hall of the memorial hall through pictures, videos and precious collections, the exhibition shows the glorious course of Sichuan oil and gas industry from scratch and development under the care of the CPC and state leaders.

四川

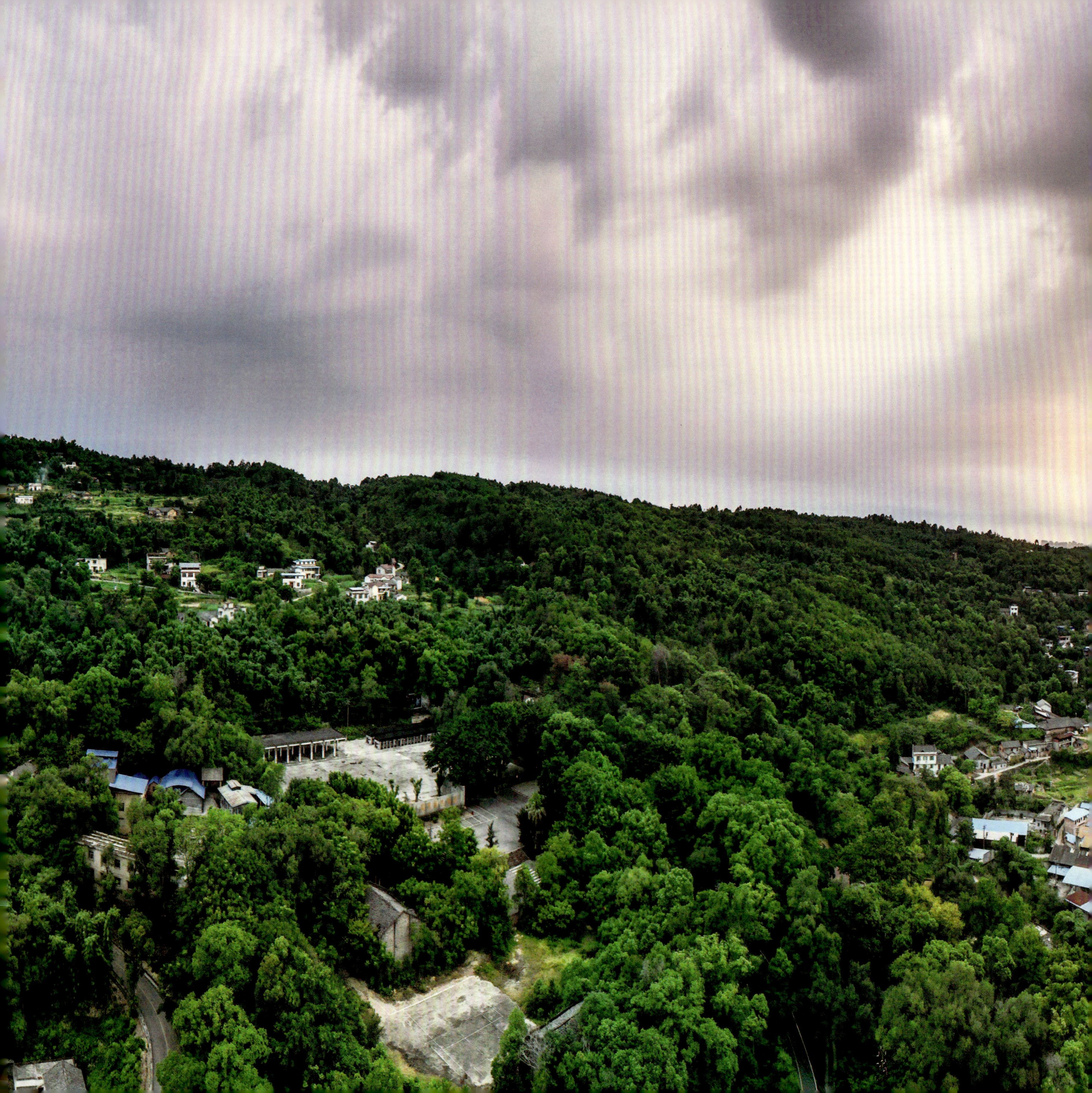

隆昌气矿圣灯山气田旧址全景。
The panoramic view of former site of Shengdeng Mountain Gas Field in Longchang Gas Mine.

国家工业遗产（第三批）

核工业受控核聚变实验旧址

我国核聚变科学家的摇篮
Cradle for Nuclear Fusion Scientists in Our Country

壹：遗产春秋
Section one: History

核工业受控核聚变实验装置旧址始建于1971年，隶属三线军工单位核工业西南物理研究院（以下简称"核西物"），是中国"四五"计划的一号工程项目，简称451工程。1987年，该工程建成的"中国环流器一号装置"获得国家科技进步一等奖，达到同类装置的国际水平。这是自主创新、科技强国的体现，增强了民族自信心和自豪感。

Original Site of Controlled Nuclear Fusion Experiment of Nuclear Industry was built in 1971. It was affiliated to Southwest Physics Research Institute of Nuclear Industry (SPRINI), the third-front military-industrial unit. It was the first project of China's "fourth five-year plan", which was abbreviated as Project No.451. In 1987, "China Circulator Device One", completed by the project and reaching the international level, won the first prize of National Scientific and Technological Progress. The device was the embodiment of independent innovation and of scientific and technological power; it also enhanced national confidence and pride.

核工业受控核聚变实验装置旧址是我国核聚变科学家的摇篮，在其服役期间培养了一大批从事受控核聚变研究的专家，如李正武先生（中国科学院院士）及潘垣先生（中国工程院院士）等。该旧址蕴含丰富的工业文化内涵，三线军工文化特点鲜明。作为我国军工行业的缩影之一，该旧址呈现出20世纪六七十年代在一穷二白基础上，开创中国受控核聚变事业，熔铸的"艰苦奋斗，奋发图强"的"三线精神"，也彰显了西南核工业人始终践行的"事业高于一切，责任重于一切，严细融入一切，进取成就一切"的核工业精神。

Original Site of Controlled Nuclear Fusion Experiment of Nuclear Industry was the cradle for nuclear fusion scientists in China. It nurtured a large number of experts in controlled nuclear fusion research, such as Mr. Li Zhengwu (Academician Chinese Academy of Science) and Mr. Pan Yuan (Academician Chinese Academy of Engineering). The original site reflected rich industrial culture and distinctive third-front military culture. As the one of epitome of China's military industry, the original site showed that China's controlled nuclear fusion cause grew out of "poverty and blankness" in the 1960s and the 1970s. The third-front spirit of "hard work with stamina and diligence" echoed with nuclear industry spirit: SPRINI workers' practice of "give priority to work, attach importance to responsibility, meticulous about every detail, aspiring at every aspect".

遗产名称/位置：核工业受控核聚变实验旧址/四川省乐山市
Heritage item/Location: Original Site of Controlled Nuclear Fusion Experiment of Nuclear Industry /Leshan City, Sichuan Province

贰：核心物项
Section two: Core items

　　451 主机大厅、控制室、电机大楼、工程实验室、整流大楼，303 大厅，实验工厂主车间及机加工设备；中国环流器一号实验装置，反场箍缩环形实验装置，预试环流器实验装置，微型环流器实验装置；李正武院士档案，何成逊先生捐赠图书资料与手绘稿。

　　451 main engine hall, control center, electrical building, engineering laboratory, rectifier building, 303 hall, main workshop and machining equipments of experimental factory; China circulator Device No.1, circular experimental device of reversed field pinch, experimental device of pre-test circulator, experimental device of micro circulator; Li Zhengwu Academician's archives, books and manuscripts donated by Mr. He Chengxun.

建设中的 451 主机大厅。
451 main engine hall under construction.

核工业受控核聚变实验装置旧址。
Original Site of Controlled Nuclear Fusion Experiment of Nuclear Industry.

451 工程实验室现状。
Current situation of 451 engineering laboratory.

国家工业遗产（第三批）

20世纪70年代钱学森与工作人员合影。
Group photo of Qian Xuesen with workers in the 1970s.

王淦昌等科学家参观合影。
Group photo of scientists including Wang Ganchang visiting the factory.

303实验大楼。
303 experimental building.

遗产名称 / 位置：核工业受控核聚变实验旧址 / 四川省乐山市
Heritage item/Location: Original Site of Controlled Nuclear Fusion Experiment of Nuclear Industry /Leshan City, Sichuan Province

四川

中国环流器一号装置安装场景。这是中国第一个跟国际主流接轨的受控核聚变装置，该装置首次将大型变压器、大型真空室及大型纵场线圈等运用到托克马克实验装置中。中国通过环流器一号实验装置的设计、建设和运行，产生了一些领先国际、国内的科学技术，如超声分子束注入技术，已在国际上广泛应用。

Installation scene of China Circulator Device No.1. This was the first controlled nuclear fusion device in China that meet international standard. The device applied large transformers, large vacuum chambers and large vertical coils into Tokamak experimental device for the first time. Through the design, construction and operation of China Circulator Device No.1, China has produced some advanced science and technology at home and aboard, such as ultrasonic molecular beam injection technology, widely used worldwide.

中国环流器一号实验装置现状。2002年，核西物在成都建成中国环流器二号实验装置。中国环流器一号实验装置正式退役。

Status quo of China Circulator Device No.1. In 2002, SPRINI completed China Circulator Device No.2. Thereafter China Circulator Device No.1 was officially out of use.

叁：遗产活化
Section three: Revitalization

　　核工业西南物理研究院通过馆史陈列保护、工业遗产实物征集、研学基地建设和党性教育基地建设等方式对旧址实施保护和利用。2012年，该旧址建成中国核聚变博物馆，目前已成为四川省科普基地、全国核科普教育基地。

　　SPRINI protects and uses the old site through exhibition and protection of museum history, collection of material objects of industrial heritage, construction of research base and construction of the party education base. In 2012, the original site was built into the museum of China nuclear fusion. At present, it has become a science popularization base in Sichuan Province and a national nuclear education base.

　　从2012年开始，中国核聚变博物馆每年接待4 000多名学生开展工程素质课；组织四川省科技活动周、征文比赛、演讲、"核你在一起"科普大赛等，吸引广大师生参与，传播军工文化精髓。

　　Since 2012, more than 4 000 students have been receiving engineering quality classes at the China Nuclear Fusion Museum. There are also activities as Sichuan Province Science and Technology Activities Week, essay competition, speech, science contest of "Nuclear with You", which have attracted the majority of teachers and students to participate in the dissemination of the essence of military culture.

中国核聚变博物馆内的两弹元勋浮雕。
Sculpture of the founding father of two-bomb in China Nuclear Fusion Museum.

中国核聚变博物馆的馆藏文物展示。特别是李正武院士的遗物，包括竺可桢亲笔签名的证明书、钱学森书信、从美国带回的打字机等，颇具收藏价值。

Display of cultural relics in China Nuclear Fusion Museum, in particular, the relics of academician Li Zhengwu, including the autographed certificate of Zhu Kezhen, letters of Qian Xuesen, typewriter brought back from the United States, which are of great collection value.

国家工业遗产（第三批）

嘉阳煤矿老矿区

中国近现代煤炭工业发展的典型缩影
Typical Miniature of China's Modern Coal Industry Development

壹：遗产春秋
Section one: History

　　成立于1938年的中英合资嘉阳煤矿，是抗日战争时期国民政府在四川大后方开办的"四大抗战煤矿"之一。1950年年初，嘉阳煤矿更名为中央直属统配406煤矿，1958年下放四川省人民政府管理，发挥了政治经济、采煤技术等引领示范作用，为四川省社会经济发展做出了重要贡献。

　　Founded in 1938, Sino-British joint venture Jiayang Coal Mine was one of the "four major Anti-Japanese War coal mines" founded by the National Government in Sichuan during the War of Resistance Against Japan Aggression. At the begins of 1950s, Jiayang Coal Mine was renamed as 406 Coal Mine directly under central management. In 1958, it was decentralized to Sichuan Provincial People's Government. Jiayang Coal Mine played a leading role in political economy and coal mining technology, and made important contributions to social economic development of Sichuan.

传统铁路运输工具。
Transport tools of traditional railway.

遗产名称／位置：嘉阳煤矿老矿区／四川省乐山市
Heritage item/Location: Old Mining Area of Jiayang Coal Mine/Leshan City, Sichuan Province

  嘉阳小火车作为世界罕见的正常运行的窄轨蒸汽客运小火车，传承了蒸汽工业文明，被称为"工业革命活化石"。黄村井作为中国典型薄煤层厚矸开采矿井，保留了北方典型的竖井提升和煤炭开采方式，是研究煤矿开采技术，进行文化创作的重要场所。嘉阳煤矿80多年艰苦创业史，是中国近代和现代煤炭工业发展的典型缩影，具有悠久的历史价值和丰厚的工业文化底蕴。

  Jiayang mini train, the world's rare steam-driven passenger train with narrow gauge, passes on steam industry civilization and is titled as "living fossil of industrial revolution". Huangcun Well with thin coal seam but thick dunn bass, typical in China, retains the shaft lifting and coal mining methods, typical in the north. Thus it is an important place to study coal mining technology and to carry out cultural creation. Jiayang Coal Mine with a history of over 80 years of hard work and rich industrial culture, is a typical miniature of China's modern coal industry development.

贰：核心物项
Section two: Core items

  黄村井，行政办公楼，大礼堂，专家楼6栋，矿工排房6栋；芭石窄轨铁路；蒸汽机车机头 ZN_{16-4} 五辆。

Huangcun Well, Administrative Building, Auditorium, 6 Expert Building, 6 Miners' Row House, Bashi narrow-gauge railway, 5 Steam Engine heads Zn_{16-4}.

嘉阳小火车科普体验基地收藏的英国老式蒸汽动力车床。
Old British steam-powered lathes, collection of Jiayang mini train science popularization base.

目前仍在运行的嘉阳小火车。
Jiayang Mini Train still in operation.

叁：遗产活化
Section three: Revitalization

中国煤炭博物馆四川嘉阳馆内薄煤层开采技术展区。
Exhibition area of thin coal seam mining technology in Sichuan Jiayang Museum of China Coal Museum.

游客在中国煤炭博物馆四川嘉阳馆内乘坐荡悠悠的矿工猴儿车。
Visitors took a ride in the miner's dangling wagon at Sichuan Jiayang Museum of China Coal Museum.

　　2004年开始，嘉阳集团公司对嘉阳小火车和芭石铁路全面彻底治理，确保安全运行。同时，挖掘抗战文化，把关闭20年之久的黄村井重新打开维修，建成体验观光煤矿，成为科普教育和爱国主义教育的亮点项目；建成中国煤炭博物馆四川嘉阳馆、中国铁道博物馆嘉阳小火车科普体验基地；对芭蕉沟工业矿区特色建筑进行保护性维修，形成风格迥异的工业古镇。

　　Since 2004, Jiayang Group worked hard to guarantee the safe operation of Jiayang mini train and Bashi Railway in an all-round way. At the same time, Jiayang Group dug into the Anti-Japanese War culture, reopened the Huangcun Well, closed for 20 years, and built it into a sightseeing coal mine, which has become a highlighted project of science popularization and patriotism education. Jiayang Group also built Sichuan Jiayang Museum of China Coal Museum and Jiayang Mini Train science popularization base of China Railway Museum. It also carried out preservation-oriented maintenance of the characteristic buildings in Bajiaogou industrial mining area to construct a distinctive industrial town.

　　通过工业遗产的保护和开发，嘉阳煤矿老矿区目前已形成了工业文化魅力独特、工业旅游亮点突出的工业遗产活化项目。

　　Through the protection and development of industrial heritages, old mining Area of Jiayang Coal Mine has now built an industrial heritage revitalization project of unique industrial cultural charm and highlighted industrial tourism.

遗产名称/位置：嘉阳煤矿老矿区/四川省乐山市
Heritage item/Location: Old Mining Area of Jiayang Coal Mine/Leshan City, Sichuan Province

四川

由苏式建筑改造而成的中国煤炭博物馆四川嘉阳馆。
Sichuan Jiayang Museum of China Coal Museum transformed from Russian-style architecture.

国家工业遗产（第三批）

嘉阳小火车。
Jiayang Mini Train.

芭蕉沟工业古镇是嘉阳小火车位于大山深处的终点站,图为芭蕉沟工业古镇主体航拍。
Bajiaogou Industrial Town is the final stop of Jiayang Mini Train deep in the mountain. This is the aerial picture of Bajiaogou Industrial Town.

国家工业遗产（第三批）

六枝矿区

煤矿三线建设的典型缩影
Typical Miniature of Coal Mine Third-Front Construction

壹：遗产春秋
Section one: History

六枝矿区工业遗址位于中国"凉都"贵州六盘水六枝特区，始建于20世纪60年代。1964年6月，国家计委、煤炭工业部派人到贵州省进行煤炭工业开发建设筹备。1964年11月，煤炭工业部发出《关于成立西南煤矿建设指挥部的通知》。1965年1月1日，西南煤矿建设指挥部在六枝正式成立。

The industrial site of Liuzhi mining area, located in Liuzhi Special Zone of Liupanshui City, Guizhou Province, "Cool Capital" of China, was constructed in the 1960s. In June 1964, the State Planning Commission and the Ministry of Coal Industry sent technicians to Guizhou province to develop and construct coal industry. In November 1964, the Ministry of Coal Industry issued the *Notice on the Establishment of Southwest Coal Mine Construction Headquarter*. On January 1st, 1965, the Southwest Coal Mine Construction Headquarter was officially established in Liuzhi.

六枝矿区的建设历程体现了"艰苦创业、勇于创新、团结协作、无私奉献"的"三线精神"。通过工业遗存老铁路、矿硐、选煤走廊、干打垒住房、苏式建筑、锻工房、木架构站台、老厂房等，既能看到工业美学元素，又能感知艰苦创业的时代精神。

The construction of Liuzhi Mining Area embodies the "third-front spirit" of "hard work, bold innovation, solid cooperation, selfless dedication". One can not only see elements of industrial aesthetics, but also perceive the time spirit of hard work through such industrial heritages as the old railway, mine pits, coal-picking corridors, adobe housing, Russian-style construction, forging workshops, wooden platforms and old factory buildings.

遗产名称 / 位置：六枝矿区 / 贵州省六盘水市
Heritage item/Location: Liuzhi Mining Area / Liupanshui City, Guizhou Province

贵州

六枝矿区选煤厂全景图。
Panorama of coal-picking plant of Liuzhi Mining Area.

国家工业遗产
（第三批）

贰：核心物项
Section two: Core items

地宗选煤厂原（精）煤运输走廊，装（卸）煤仓，洗选车间，地宗煤矿主井硐，职工澡堂；六枝煤矿主副井硐，四角田煤矿主井硐，生产连（区）队办公区，矿锻工房，筒子楼，职工干打垒成片住房，职工大食堂，苏式办公楼与礼堂；地宗铁路专用线及補林大桥，物资总仓库木架构站台，火工品库，六枝电厂老厂房、除尘等附属设施。

Raw (fine) coal transport corridor of Dizong coal-picking plant, loading (unloading) coal bunker, washing workshop, main well pit of Dizong Coal Mine, staff bathhouse, main and auxiliary well pits of Liuzhi Coal Mine, main well pit of Sijiaotian Coal Mine, production company office, mine forging workshops, tube-shaped apartment, workers' adobe housing, staff canteen, Soviet-style office building and auditorium, Dizong railway special line and Bulin Bridge, wooden structure platform of Material Warehouse, Fireworks Warehouse, Old Workshop, dust removal and other ancillary facilities of Liuzhi Power Plant.

选煤厂远景
Close shot of coal-picking plant.

遗产名称 / 位置：六枝矿区 / 贵州省六盘水市
Heritage item/Location: Liuzhi Mining Area / Liupanshui City, Guizhou Province

四角田煤矿办公楼。
Office Building of Sijiaotian Coal Mine.

四角田煤矿平硐。1966 年 8 月四角田矿整体开发建设，于 2013 年实施关闭转移。
Footrill of Sijiaotian Coal Mine. In August 1966, Sijiaotian Coal Mine was put into construction, and in 2013, it was closed and shifted.

贵州

国家工业遗产（第三批）

地宗铁路专用线于1965年通车，是六盘水矿区最早通车的矿区专用线，标志着六盘水地区煤炭铁路外运的开始。

Dizong Railway Special Line. It was put into operation in 1965. It was the first special line in Liupanshui Mining Area, marking the beginning of outward transportation of Liupanshui coal railway.

1964年建设的物资总仓库木架构站台，大西南"三线建设"物资仓储中转基地。车站站台全木结构，是目前贵州省保存最完整的三线物资储运火车站。

Wooden structure platform of Material Warehouse was built in 1964, transit depot of Great Southwest Third-Front Construction material storage transfer base. The entire wooden structure of the station platform is the best preserved third-front cargo storage and transportation railway station in Guizhou Province.

遗产名称 / 位置：六枝矿区 / 贵州省六盘水市
Heritage item/Location: Liuzhi Mining Area / Liupanshui City, Guizhou Province

贵州

六枝电厂是六盘水市最早建设和发电的矿区自备火电厂，1960 年 2 月安装匈牙利生产的 1 500 千瓦发电机组 1 台并发电，1960 年年底安装国产 1 500 千瓦电机组 1 台并发电，1967 年罗马尼亚生产的第三台发电机组（3 000 千瓦）建成发电。

Liuzhi Power Plant is the first-built self-supply heat-engine plant of Liupanshui City. In February 1960, the plant installed one set of 1 500 kW generator produced by Hungary and started generating electricity; at the end of 1960, the plant installed one set of domestic 1 500 kW generator and started generating electricity; in 1967, the third set of generator (3 000 kW) produced by Romania was built to generate electricity.

贵州万山汞矿

"中国汞都" 两千年的传奇
"China's Mercury Capital" Two Thousand Years of Legend

壹：遗产春秋
Section one: History

　　万山的矿业开采冶炼史始于周秦时期，汉代已闻名国内，距今已有两千多年历史。唐宋时期即掌握了以火攻取的生产技术，明代已进行规模开采。1950 年，中国调集井巷公司等中央地质勘探队勘探，探明储量 3.5 万吨，并组建省属企业湘黔汞矿公司（贵州汞矿前身）进行开采冶炼，使万山逐渐成为全国最大的汞工业生产基地，产量一度占全国汞产量的 60% 以上，被誉为"中国汞都"。

　　The mining and smelting of Wanshan Mine began in the Zhou-Qin Dynasties, and became well-known domestically in the Han Dynasty with a history of over 2 000 years. It already extracted mercury by firing in the Tang and Song Dynasties and its scale mining started in the Ming Dynasty. In 1950, the central geological prospecting team, including Jingxiang Company, was sent to explore mercury by the leadership. And the team detected 35 000 tons of mercury reserves.Thereafter, the provincial enterprise Xiangqian Mercury Mine Company (predecessor of Guizhou Mercury Mine) was established to start mining and smelting. Since then, Wanshan had gradually become the largest mercury production base in China, with its output ever exceeding 60% of the total in China, and it had been praised as the "China's Mercury Capital".

　　贵州汞矿虽在 21 世纪初关闭，但数千年汞矿开采、冶炼遗留下来的诸如仙人洞、大小洞、黑硐子、云南梯等矿业遗迹历史悠久、内涵丰富，层层叠叠长达 970 千米的地下坑道，堪称地下长城，规模宏大、世界罕见。贵州万山汞矿遗址是全国乃至世界现存开采时间早、保护利用完善的汞矿工业遗址，蕴藏着丰富的历史、文化、政治、科技、经济、社会及国际关系等多方面的价值，是人类文明创造与智慧的杰出代表，具有不可再生性。

　　Although Guizhou Mercury Mine was closed at the beginning of 21 century, the mining relics were retained after thousands of years of mercury mining and smelting. Such relics as Xianren Adit, Big and Small Adits, Black Adit and Yunnan Ladder have long history and provoke rich conception. The sophisticated 970-kilometer-long underground tunnel, with such large scale rarely seen worldwide, can be called "Underground Great Wall". The non-renewable Wanshan Mercury Mine of Guizhou Site is an industrial site with early mining time and perfect protection and utilization in China and even in the world. It contains rich values in history, culture, politics, science and technology, economy, society and international relations, and is an outstanding representative of the creation and wisdom of human civilization.

遗产名称/位置：贵州万山汞矿/贵州省铜仁市
Heritage item/Location: Wanshan Mercury Mine of Guizhou/Tongren City, Guizhou Province

贰：核心物项
Section two: Core items

黑硐子，仙人洞，云南梯主硐口，300吨机选厂，冶炼厂冶炼炉车间，贵州汞矿科学文化中心，大礼堂，苏联专家楼，万山特区商店，医院门诊大楼，劳动服务中心，技工学校，职工食堂，百货商店，电影院，粮店。

Black Adit, Xianren Adit, the main adit of Yunnan Ladder, 300-ton mechanical concentrator, smelter workshops of smelting plant, Guizhou Mercury Mine science and culture center, auditorium, Soviet Union expert building, Wanshan Special Zone store, hospital outpatient building, labor service center, technical school, staff canteen, department store, cinema, grain store.

贵州

云南梯主硐口。
The main adit of Yunnan ladder.

国家工业遗产（第三批）

苏联专家楼。20世纪50年代初，地质部和冶金部为加强在万山矿区的地质工作，曾聘请苏联地质专家帮助工作，专门修建了四幢欧式建筑用来接待苏联专家。

Soviet Union expert building. In the early 1950s, in order to strengthen the geological work in the Wanshan mining area, the Ministry of Geology and the Ministry of Metallurgy employed Soviet geologists to assist the work. Four European style buildings were specially built to receive Soviet geologists.

遗产名称/位置：贵州万山汞矿/贵州省铜仁市
Heritage item/Location: Wanshan Mercury Mine of Guizhou/Tongren City, Guizhou Province

贵州

冶炼厂冶炼炉车间。
Smelter Workshops of Smelting Plant.

300 吨机选厂。
300-ton Mechanical Concentrator.

叁：遗产活化
Section three: Revitalization

近年来，矿区将原来的贵州汞矿矿部办公大楼改建成万山汞矿工业遗产博物馆。曾经的汞矿中枢、发号施令的地方现在变成了静静的展厅，展厅设有万山汞矿沙盘模型、形象墙，并陈列了万山汞矿采冶历史及产品，从汞矿开采、冶炼、炼丹及英法水银公司成立直至关闭等的兴衰过程，突显了万山汞矿遗址独有的工业文化内涵。

In recent years, the original office building of Guizhou Mercury Mine has been transformed into the Wanshan Mercury Mine Industrial Heritage Museum. The mercury minecenter, source of all orders, now has become a quiet exhibition hall, where there are the mine's sand table model, image wall, and the mining and smelting history and products ranging from the mercury mining, smelting, refining, to the establishment and closure of the Anglo-French mercury company. Each carries and reflects the unique industrial culture of Wanshan Mercury Mine.

万山汞矿工业遗产博物馆。
Wanshan Mercury Mine Industrial Heritage Museum.

遗产名称/位置：贵州万山汞矿/贵州省铜仁市
Heritage item/Location: Wanshan Mercury Mine of Guizhou/Tongren City, Guizhou Province

贵州

中国汞都·国家矿山公园。2009年贵州万山汞矿遗址被命名国家公园，总体规划面积105平方千米，是贵州省唯一的国家矿山公园，展现给人们的是有关汞工业文明的深厚历史、历代矿工的智慧和血汗凝聚成的精神高地。

China's Mercury Capital · National Mining Park. In 2009, Wanshan Mercury Mine of Guizhou Site was named as the National Mining Park with a total planning area of 105 square kilometers. It is the only national mining park in Guizhou Province, showing the grand history of mercury industrial civilization and the wisdom and sweat of miners in previous dynasties.

国家工业遗产（第三批）

云南省凤庆茶厂老厂区

国家级工夫名茶"滇红"诞生地
National Gongfu Famous Tea "Dian Hong" birthplace

壹：遗产春秋
Section one: History

云南省凤庆茶厂（云南滇红集团老厂区），是我国驰名中外的名茶"滇红"的诞生地。1938年，冯绍裘作为中茶公司技师到顺宁考察，成功试制出红茶、绿茶两种样茶，从此开创了顺宁茶叶精制的历史。1939年3月，由冯绍裘主持，建立了云南中国茶叶贸易股份有限公司顺宁实验茶厂。1954年改为"云南凤庆茶厂"，1996年整体改制为"云南滇红集团股份有限公司"（以下简称"滇红集团"）。

Yunnan Fengqing Tea Factory (the old factory of Yunnan Dian Hong Group) is the birthplace of the famous tea "Dian Hong". In 1938, the technician of Chinese Tea Company Feng Shaoqiu went for an inspection in Shunning, and he successfully tried out black tea and green tea. From then on, Fen Shaoqiu started the history of making refined Shunning tea. In March 1939, Feng Shaoqiu presided over the establishment of Yunnan China Tea Trade Co., Ltd. Shunning Experimental Tea Factory. In 1954, it was renamed as "Yunnan Fengqing Tea Factory". In 1996, it was transformed into "Yunnan Dian Hong Group Co., Ltd."(Dianhong Group).

云南省凤庆茶厂既是"滇红"的诞生地，又是"滇红"工夫毛茶、红碎茶两个毛茶收购标准样和滇红工夫茶、红碎茶两个加工验收统一标准样的国家一套样制样单位。目前，滇红集团保存有始于1953年的历史实物样茶4 967件（筒）。

Yunnan Fengqing Tea Factory in Yunnan Province is the birthplace of "Dianhong", it is also a set of sample preparation units of two standard samples of "Dianhong" Gongfu Tea and black broken tea, and two standard samples of "Dianhong" Gongfu Tea and black broken tea. At present, Dianhong Group has preserved 4 967 pieces (drums) of historical samples of tea dating back to 1953.

遗产名称 / 位置：云南省凤庆茶厂老厂区 / 云南省临沧市凤庆县
Heritage item/Location: Yunnan Fengqing Tea Old Factory Area/ Fengqing County, Lincang City, Yunnan Province

茶厂主产"凤"牌滇红茶，曾作为国礼赠送英国女王伊丽莎白二世、斯里兰卡总理等多国政要。下辖的茶叶科学研究院有着40年的历史，茶树良种资源圃征集保存了1 500多份茶树育种材料，保存有世界各地800多个茶树优良品种，被誉为世界茶树种质基因库。

The tea factory's star product "phoenix" brand black tea was sent as a national ceremony gift to foreign dignitaries as Queen Elizabeth II and Sri Lanka's prime minister. The Institute of Tea Science under its jurisdiction has a history of 40 years. The tea tree improved-variety garden has collected and preserved over 1 500 breeding materials and over 800 types of tea trees around the world. It is therefore known as the world's tea tree germplasm.

目前，滇红集团拥有10万亩茶园基地，其中2万亩通过了欧美及美国有机茶认证、1 050亩通过了中国有机茶认证等，拥有初制加工厂85个（三位一体改革为21个茶场），精制加工厂占地340亩，年生产能力1.5万吨。

At present, Dian Hong Group has 100 thousand mu of tea garden base, of which 20 thousand mu has certification of European and American organic tea, and 1.05 thousand mu has certification of Chinese organic tea. Dianhong Group comprises 85 initial processing plants (21 tea farms after trinity reform) and 340 mu of refined processing plant with an annual production capacity of 15 thousand tons.

"滇红茶"创始人冯绍裘铜像。
Bronze statue of Feng Shaoqiu, founder of "Dianhong" Tea.

云南

国家工业遗产（第三批）

贰：核心物项
Section two: Core items

　　苏式建筑办公楼，冯绍裘铜像，烘干、筛分、成品、制箱、包装车间，仓库3栋；铁轨3段；1975年德国进口500HW低速柴油发电机，1975年购置的解放牌消防车，精制茶生产线，木制匀堆机2套，风选机；冯式"三桶式手揉机""脚踏与动力两用之揉茶机""脚踏与动力两用之烘茶机"黑白照片。

Russian-style office building, bronze statue of Feng Shaoqiu, packaging workshops of drying, screening, final products, boxing, 3 warehouses; 3 segments of the track ; 500HW low-speed diesel generator imported from Germany in 1975, fire truck of "Liberation" brand purchased in 1975, production line of refined tea, 2 sets of wooden stacking machine, wind machine, black-and-white photos of Feng-style "three-barrel hand kneading machine", "tea kneading machine driven by pedal and power" and "tea curing machine driven by pedal and power".

1953—2000年历史实物样茶4 967件（筒）。
4 967 pieces of sample tea from 1953 to 2000.

1975年从德国进口的500HW低速柴油发电机。
500HW low-speed diesel generator imported from Germany in 1975.

252

遗产名称 / 位置：云南省凤庆茶厂老厂区 / 云南省临沧市凤庆县
Heritage item/Location: Yunnan Fengqing Tea Old Factory Area/ Fengqing County, Lincang City, Yunnan Province

凤庆茶厂 1975 年购置的解放牌消防车。
Fire truck of "Liberation" brand purchased for Fengqing Tea Factory in 1975.

半机械式制茶设备。
Self-made tea-making device.

20 世纪 50 年代建盖的苏式建筑办公楼。
Russian-style office buildings in the 1950s.

云南

253

国家工业遗产
（第三批）

20世纪50年代建盖的成品车间。
Final product's workshop built in the 1950s.

象征着工业文明进程的铁轨，将各生产车间及传统工夫红茶仓库连在一起。
Railway, symbolizing industrial civilization, links production workshops with traditional Gongfu Black Tea warehouse.

遗产名称/位置：云南省凤庆茶厂老厂区/云南省临沧市凤庆县
Heritage item/Location: Yunnan Fengqing Tea Old Factory Area/ Fengqing County, Lincang City, Yunnan Province

叁：遗产活化
Section three: Revitalization

茶厂展览馆，接待参观，展示文化。
Exhibition Room, reception and the tea culture show.

云南

国家工业遗产（第三批）

羊八井地热发电试验设施

中国自主研制的首台千瓦级地热发电机组
China's First Kilowatt Geothermal Generating Set

壹：遗产春秋
Section one: History

羊八井地热发电试验设施（1 000千瓦）试验机组位于西藏当雄县羊八井镇西部，1977年9月并网发电成功，1985年顺利完成实验工作使命，退出运行，标志着我国地热发电技术在实际应用中的日趋成熟。

Test set of Yangbajing Geothermal Power Test Facility (1 000 KW) is located in the west of Yangbajing Town in Dangxiong County, Tibet. It was successfully connected to the grid in September 1977, completed the experiment mission in 1985 and was out of operation. This marked the increasing maturity of the practical application of geothermal power generation technology in China.

羊八井地热发电试验设施是1977年开发西藏羊八井地热资源过程中并网发电的第一台1 000千瓦试验机组，也是中国自主研制的第一台千瓦级地热发电机组，拉开了中国在高海拔、利用浅层地热资源发电的序幕。

Yangbajing Geothermal Power Test Facility is the first 1 000 KW test set connected to the grid in the process of developing the geothermal resources of Tibet Yangbajing Well in 1977; it was also the first kilowatt-scale geothermal generator set developed by China; it ushered in the use of shallow geothermal resources to generate electricity at the high elevation in China.

运行一站远景。
Distant view of Function Station 1.

遗产名称 / 位置：羊八井地热发电试验设施 / 西藏自治区拉萨市
Heritage item/Location: Yangbajing Geothermal Power Test Facility/ Lhasa City, Tibet Autonomous Region

贰：核心物项
Section two: Core items

试验机厂房；汽轮机，汽轮发电机，行车，扩容器，冷凝器，射水抽气器，水泵3台，配电盘柜6个。

Test set plant, steam turbine, steam turbine generator, bridge crane, flash tank, condenser, hydraulic air pump, 3 water pumps, 6 switchboard cabinets.

1兆瓦地热试验汽轮机冷凝器。
Condenser of 1 MW geothermal test turbine.

1兆瓦地热试验汽轮机组。
Test set of 1 MW geothermal turbine.

1兆瓦地热试验汽轮机组主厂房。
Main Plant of test set of 1 MW of geothermal turbine.

西藏

叁：遗产今夕
Section three: Current Situation

羊八井1 000千瓦试验机组的试运成功，为我国地热事业研发提供了基础资料，积累了大量的实验数据，培养了技术人才。如今，它虽然静静地躺在一号机房内，但它的贡献不可磨灭，它的历史更值得被永远铭记。

The successful operation of Yangbajing 1 000 KW test machine provided basic data for the research and development of geothermal cause in China. With a large amount of experimental data, it nurtured technical personnel. Although it stays quietly in workshop 1 now, its contribution is indelible. It was written into history to be remembered forever.

运行一站鸟瞰，黄色建筑为1号机组厂房。
Aeroview of Function Station 1. The yellow building is the plant of machine set 1.

遗产名称 / 位置：羊八井地热发电试验设施 / 西藏自治区拉萨市
Heritage item/Location: Yangbajing Geothermal Power Test Facility/ Lhasa City, Tibet Autonomous Region

西藏

地热井口。Geothermal wellhead.

热网管道。Hot-supply pipes.

国家工业遗产（第三批）

红光沟航天六院旧址

中国航天动力之乡：液体火箭发动机研制基地
Hometown of China's Aerodynamic Power : Liquid Rocket Engine Development Base

壹：遗产春秋
Section one: History

红光沟航天部第六研究院（简称航天六院）旧址位于陕西省宝鸡市凤县凤州镇，创建于1965年，是我国"三线建设"时期唯一的液体火箭发动机研制基地。

Located in Fengzhou Town, Fengxian County, Baoji City, Shanxi Province, the former site of the Sixth Research Institute of Hongguanggou Aerospace is the only liquid rocket engine development base in China during the Third-Front construction period.

在这里研制的各型号发动机，圆满完成了以"两弹一星""载人航天""探月工程""北斗导航"等为代表的国家重大航天工程任务。我国目前在轨运行的200多颗卫星等航天器，都是由这里研发的发动机送入太空的，其中，远程火箭一级发动机获得国家金质奖，是当之无愧的"金牌发动机"，这里因此被誉为"中国航天动力之乡"。

Various types of engines developed here have successfully completed major national space engineering tasks, such as "two bombs and one satellite", "manned spaceflight", "lunar exploration project" and "Beidou navigation". China's more than 200 satellites and other spacecraft in orbit are launched into space by the engines developed here. Among them, the first stage engine of long-range rocket won the national gold medal, which is worthy of the "gold medal engine". Therefore, it is known as the "hometown of China's aerospace power".

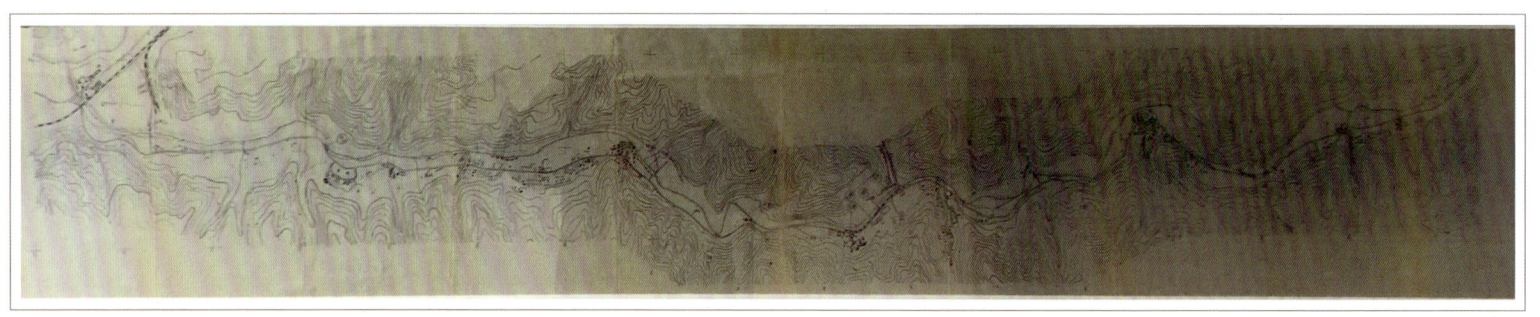

红光沟航天六院旧址总体分布手绘图。
Hand drawn map of the overall distribution of the former site of the Sixth Research Institute of Hongguanggou Aerospace.

遗产名称/位置：红光沟航天六院旧址/陕西省宝鸡市凤县
Heritage item/Location: Former Site of the Sixth Research Institute of Hongguanggou Aerospace /Feng County, Baoji City, Shaanxi Province

陕西

亚洲最大的常规液体火箭发动机一号试车台。
No.1 test bed, the largest in Asia, for conventional liquid rocket engine.

近年来，红光沟航天六院高度重视红光沟航天六院旧址的保护与利用，开展了一系列面向领导干部、青年员工、骨干职工及各大高校的爱国主义教育和航天精神教育，为传承和弘扬航天精神发挥了重要作用。未来将以旧址为依托，建设突出航天、三线、红色文化的全国性教育培训基地，建成国家级航天精神文化区。

In recent years, the Sixth Aerospace Research Institute has attached great importance to the protection and utilization of the former site of the Sixth Research Institute of Hongguanggou Aerospace. It has carried out a series of patriotism education and space spirit education for leading cadres, young employees, key staff and universities, which have played an important role in inheriting and carrying forward the aerospace spirit. In the future, based on the former site, a national education and training base highlighting aerospace, third-front and red culture will be built to become a national aerospace spiritual and cultural zone.

贰：核心物项
Section two: Core items

科研楼，机要室，行政后勤楼，力学试验室、"厕所"试验室，201 洞，小泵试验室，张贵田院士之家，科研区 1 号、2 号专家楼，红光工人俱乐部，指挥部办公楼，大礼堂，招待所；红光沟航天六院旧址总体分布手绘图等历史档案及口述历史材料。

Scientific research building, confidential room, administrative & logistics building, mechanical laboratory, "toilet" laboratory, 201 adit, small pump laboratory, Academician Zhang Guitian's house, No.1 and No.2 expert buildings in the scientific research area, Hongguang Workers' Club, headquarters building, auditorium, guest house; historical archives and oral historical materials hand drawing of the overall distribution of the Sixth Research Institute of Hongguanggou Aerospace.

"厕所"实验室。1970 年，在研制试验条件不具备，而型号任务又迫在眉睫的情况下，科研人员利用暂时没用的厕所改装成小发动机研制试验室，先后进行了数十台次、上万次热启动试验。我国首台单组元姿态控制发动机就在此诞生，为我国战略战术导弹和宇航运载做出重要贡献。

"Toilet" laboratory. In 1970, when the conditions for development and test were not prepared, and the task of model was urgent, researchers converted the unused toilet beside the creek into a simple small engine development laboratory, where dozens of engines and tens of thousands of hot start tests were carried out successively. China's first single—componentattitude control engine was born here, making important contributions to China's strategic and tactical missiles and aerospace transportation.

遗产名称 / 位置：红光沟航天六院旧址 / 陕西省宝鸡市凤县
Heritage item/Location: Former Site of the Sixth Research Institute of Hongguanggou Aerospace /Feng County, Baoji City, Shaanxi Province

陕西

201洞洞口。创建于1971年，是红光沟航天六院旧址"三大重点"工程之一，被称之为"201洞"。现已作为学习航天专家、首任主任杨敏达带领下形成的"艰苦奋斗、无私奉献"精神的重要教学点。

Entrance of 201 adit. Built in 1971, it was one of the former site's three key projects code-named "201" project, so commonly known as "201 adit". Now it has become an important field teaching point to learn the spirit of "hard work and selfless dedication" formed under the leadership of Yang Minda, an aerospace expert and the first director of "201 adit".

试验区201洞外小泵试验室。创建于1972年，是红光沟航天六院旧址小型泵水力试验室。一层为试验区、二层为室领导办公室区。航天专家、"201洞"首任主任杨敏达曾在此办公。

Small pump laboratory outside the 201 adit in experimental area. Built in 1972, it was the small pump laboratory of the former site of the Sixth Research Institute of Hongguanggou Aerospace. The first floor is the experimental area, and the second floor is the office area of office leaders. Yang Minda, an aerospace expert and the first director of "201 adit", once worked here.

国家工业遗产（第三批）

红光沟航天六院旧址指挥部大礼堂。创建于1973年，是红光沟航天六院旧址指挥部集大型会议、文艺活动、电影院等功能于一体的职工活动综合体，会场能容纳千人。
Headquarters auditorium of the former site of the Sixth Research Institute of Hongguanggou Aerospace. Built in 1973, it was a staff activity complex with functions of large-scale meetings, literary and artistic activities, cinemas and so on. It can hold about one thousand of people.

科研区力学试验室。创建于1969年，是红光沟航天六院旧址科研区航天液体火箭发动机研制的重点试验室之一。
Mechanical library in scientific research area. Built in 1969, it was one of the key laboratories in scientific research area of the former site of the Sixth Research Institute of Hongguanggou Aerospace with its mission developing aerospace liquid rocket engines.

指挥部办公楼。创建于1973年，是红光沟航天六院旧址的指挥中心与神经中枢，组织指挥了全基地的科研、生产，是航天系统工程综合管理思想的重要实践场所。
Headquarters building. Built in 1973, it was the command center and nerve center of the former site of the Sixth Research Institute of Hongguanggou Aerospace, which organizes the scientific research and production of the whole base, where comprehensive management idea of space system engineering is put into practice.

遗产名称/位置：红光沟航天六院旧址/陕西省宝鸡市凤县
Heritage item/Location: Former Site of the Sixth Research Institute of Hongguanggou Aerospace /Feng County, Baoji City, Shaanxi Province

陕西

张贵田，中国工程院院士，液体火箭发动机专家，我国液体火箭发动机技术的主要开拓者和技术带头人之一。40多年来，一直从事液体火箭发动机的研究、设计工作。在国内率先提出用液相分区方法解决发动机不稳定燃烧的难题；主持研制成功的高空发动机、双向摇摆二次启动常规高空发动机、双组元微型发动机均填补了国内空白。曾作为主要完成人之一的长征四号A运载火箭获国家科技进步特等奖1项。

Zhang Guitian, Academician of Chinese Academy of Engineering, expert of liquid rocket engine, one of the main pioneers and technology leaders of liquid rocket engine technology in China. For 40 years, he has been engaged in the research and design of liquid rocket engine. He took the lead in proposing to solve the problem of unstable combustion of engine by liquid partition method. He presided over the research and development of the high altitude engine, the conventional high altitude engine with two-way swing and two-component micro engine, which have filled in the domestic blank. He was one of the leader of the Long March 4 A carrier rocket that won a National Science and Technology Progress Award.

傅永贵，1936年12月26日出生。1963年毕业后分配到国防部第五研究院一分院十一所，从事液体火箭发动机的研制工作。1969年10月，响应国家"三线建设"的号召，来到陕西凤县红光沟，他是十一所第一个进沟的科研人员。此后的30多年，他扎根三线，潜心研究，先后参与并主持了10多个型号发动机的研制，参与靶场发射60余次。主持研制的发动机获得国家科技进步特等奖和国家质量银质奖。

Fu Yonggui, born on December 26th, 1936. After graduation in 1963, he was assigned to the 11th Institute of the first Branch of the Fifth Research Institute of the Ministry of National Defense to engage in the research and development of liquid rocket engines. In October 1969, in response to the call of the third-front movement, he came to Hongguanggou, Fengxian County, Shaanxi Province, becoming the first scientific researcher of the 11th Institute to work in Hongguanggou. Over the next 30 years, he took root in the third-front, devoted himself to research, presided over the development of more than 10 models of engines, and participated in more than 60 launches from the range. The engine he had researched anddeveloped won the national science and technology progress award and silver award of National Quality Award.

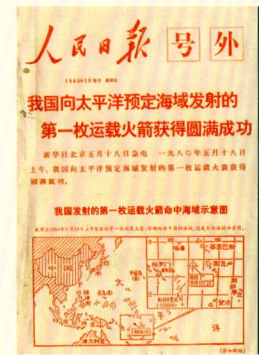

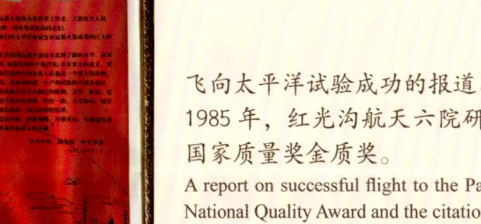

飞向太平洋试验成功的报道、国家质量奖金质奖章、嘉奖令。1985年，红光沟航天六院研发的远程火箭一级发动机获得国家质量奖金质奖。

A report on successful flight to the Pacific Ocean, medal of the Gold Award of National Quality Award and the citation. In 1985, the first stage long-range rocket engine developed by the Sixth Research Institute of Hongguanggou Aerospace won the Gold Award of National Quality Award.

中科院国家授时中心蒲城长短波授时台

新中国建设的第一个授时台
The First Time Service Platform Constructed in China

壹：遗产春秋
Section one: History

中科院国家授时中心蒲城长短波授时台遗址是新中国成立后研制建设的第一个授时台。20世纪60年代，随着我国第一颗原子弹试验成功，人造卫星和运载火箭发射对授时提出了更高的需求。1966年，国防科委批准由中国科学院牵头在陕西省关中地区筹建短波授时台，该台属"三线"单位，代号为"326工程"。

The site of Pucheng BPL&BPM National Time Service Center of Chinese Academy of Sciences was the first time service platform developed and built after the founding of China. In the 1960s, with the success of China's first atomic bomb test, the launch of satellites and carrier rockets put forward a higher demand of time service. In 1966, Science Commission for National Defense approved the Chinese Academy of Sciences to take the lead in the construction of a BPM platform in Central Shaanxi Province, a "third-front" unit with the code name of "Project 326".

20世纪70年代，为满足我国战略武器和空间技术的发展需求，1973年，经国务院、中央军委批准由中国科学院抓总，负责建设授时精度更高的长波授时台。长波授时台作为短波授时台的第二期工程，代号"3262工程"。地址选定在蒲城县城西杨庄乡。

In the 1970s, in order to meet the development needs of China's strategic weapons and space technology, the State Council and the Central Military Commission approved the Chinese Academy of Sciences to build a BPL platform with higher precision in 1973. BPL, as the second phase of BPM has a code name of "Project 3262". It was located in Xiyangzhuang Township, Pucheng County.

中科院国家授时中心蒲城长短波授时台的研制建设，涵盖了无线电技术、天文测量技术、原子频标技术、发射天线技术和电子器件材料技术等诸多方面，凝聚了20世纪60年代的中国科学院和相关部委等许多科研机构科学家的智慧和劳动，是当时中国科技发展水平的代表。

The research and development of Pucheng BPL&BPM National Time Service Center of Chinese Academy of Sciences involves radio technology, astronomical measurement technology, atomic frequency scale technology, transmitting antenna technology and electronic material technology. It unfolds the wisdom and labor of scientists from such scientific research institutions as the Chinese Academy of Sciences and the relevant ministries and commissions in the 1960s. It is the representative of the scientific and technological level of China at that time.

遗产名称/位置：中科院国家授时中心蒲城长短波授时台 / 陕西省渭南市蒲城县
Heritage item/Location: Pucheng BPL&BPM National Time Service Center of Chinese Academy of Sciences / Pucheng County, Weinan City, Shaanxi Province

贰：核心物项
Section two: Core items

金帜山短波授时台发播大厅，杨庄长波授时台地下发播大厅；短波发射机及辅助设备，长波发射机及辅助设备；四塔倒锥形长波发射天线。

Transmission hall of Jinzhishan BPM platform, underground transmission hall of Yangzhuang BPL platform; BPM transmitters and auxiliary equipments, BPL transmitters and auxiliary equipments; four-tower inverted-cone antenna.

陕西

位于蒲城唐陵山的老短波授时台旧址。
The site of the old BPM platform in Tanglingshan Mountain, Pucheng County.

国家工业遗产（第三批）

发射机水泵机组，长波授时发射机辅助设备。
Water pump of the transmitter, BPL transmitter and auxiliary equipments.

杭州无线电厂生产的天线交换开关，老短波发射机辅助设备。
An antenna switch produced by Hangzhou Radio Factory, an old BPM transmitter and auxiliary equipments.

长波台发射机辅助设备。
BPL transmitters and auxiliary equipments.

遗产名称/位置：中科院国家授时中心蒲城长短波授时台 / 陕西省渭南市蒲城县
Heritage item/Location: Pucheng BPL&BPM National Time Service Center of Chinese Academy of Sciences / Pucheng County, Weinan City, Shaanxi Province

陕西

老长波台发播大厅。长波授时台机房建筑由西北建筑设计院设计，陕西省第四建筑公司建设，曾荣获国家建筑设计奖。
Transmission hall of the old BPL platform. BPL room building was designed by Northwest Architectural Design Institute and built by Shaanxi No.4 Construction Company. It has won the National Architectural Design Award.

老短波台发播大厅。
Transmission hall of the old BPM platform.

国家工业遗产（第三批）

短波发射控制大厅。Control hall of BPM transmission.

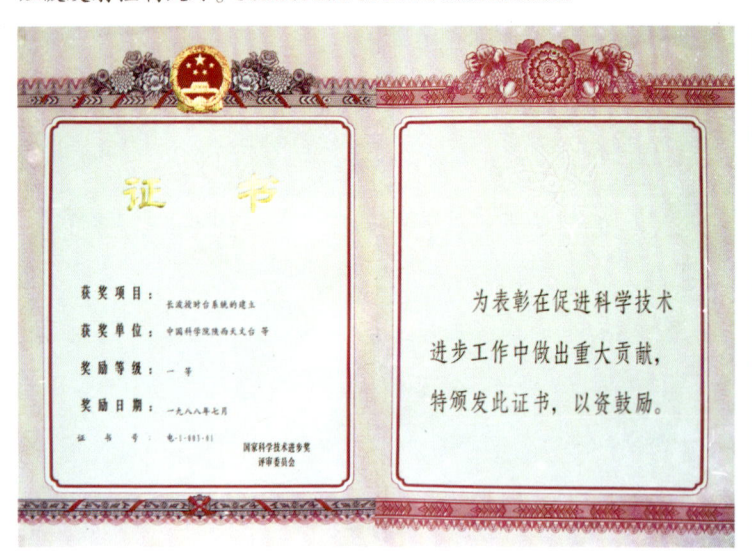

1988年"长波授时台系统的建立"获得国家科学技术进步奖一等奖。
In 1988, "The establishment of BPL system" won the First Prize of the National Science and Technology Progress Award.

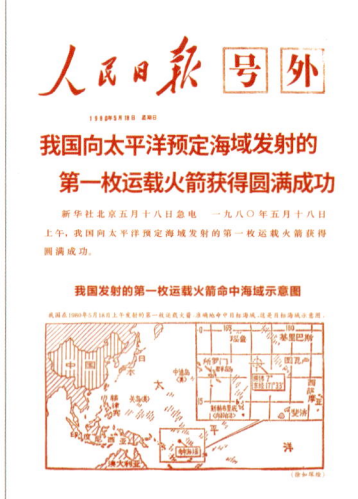

人民日报对于长短波台支撑国家任务的报道。
Report by *People's Daily* on BPL platform supporting the national mission.

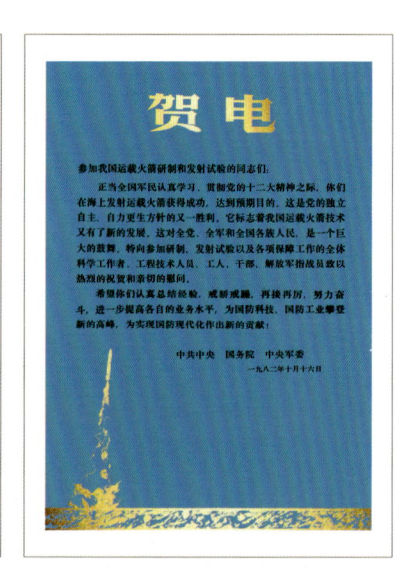

长短波台完成任务接到的贺电。
Congratulatory telegram received after the completion of a mission by BPL platform.

遗产名称/位置：中科院国家授时中心蒲城长短波授时台/陕西省渭南市蒲城县
Heritage item/Location: Pucheng BPL&BPM National Time Service Center of Chinese Academy of Sciences / Pucheng County, Weinan City, Shaanxi Province

陕西

长波授时发播天线。长波授时天线体由当时的电子工业部 1022 所设计研制，天线体呈四塔倒锥形，塔距 400 米，塔高 206 米，建筑规模庞大，是当地标志性建筑。
BPL antenna was designed and developed by the Ministry of Electronic Industry 1022 of the day. The antenna is 206 meters high, of the shape of four-tower inverted-cone, and with the tower distance of 400 meters. With a large building scale, it is a local landmark.

国家工业遗产（第三批）

定边盐场

中国"红色盐都"：陕甘边区的"中央第一财政"
China's "Red Salt City": "The First Governmentfinance Contributor" in Shaan-Gan Border Region

壹：遗产春秋
Section one: History

陕西省定边县产盐历史悠久，始于汉代，昌于隋唐，盛于明清。1934年，随着陕甘边区革命根据地的建立，第一个红色盐场陕甘边区盐场堡盐场（今延长石油定边盐化工有限公司前身）于定边县盐场堡成立。1937年陕甘宁边区政府成立后，定边盐湖作为边区政府最重要的经济来源，为中国人民艰苦卓绝的抗日战争做出了重大贡献。

Dingbian County in Shaanxi Province has a long history of salt production, which began in the Han Dynasty, flourished in the Sui and Tang Dynasties, and reached its peak in the Ming and Qing Dynasties. In 1934, the revolutionary base area in the Shaan-Gan border region was established, and then the first red saltern, Yanchangbu Saltern (the predecessor of Yanchang Petroleum Dingbian Salt Chemical Industry Company) was founded in Dingbian County. In 1937, the government of Shaan-Gan-Ning border region was established. Dingbian Salt Lake became its most important economic source and made great contributions to Chinese people's arduous War of Resistance Against Japan.

定边盐化厂办公楼遗址
Dingbian Salt Chemical Plant office building site.

遗产名称/位置：定边盐场/陕西省榆林市定边县
Heritage item/Location: Dingbian Saltern/Dingbian County, Yulin City, Shaanxi Province

新中国成立后，定边盐场发扬优良传统，于1953年逐渐恢复老湖打盐及盐田生产。1960年，定边盐场收归地方管理，成立定边盐化厂并逐渐发展成为县域经济支柱企业。2001年，定边盐化厂改制为定边县长城盐化有限责任公司。经过定边盐场几代人的努力，定边盐场"埋头苦干、开拓创新"的企业精神薪火相传，以盐湖红色旅游为基础的国家工业遗产保护利用工程，将促使千年盐湖再展新姿。

After the founding of the People's Republic of China, Dingbian Saltern gradually resumed its production in Dingbian Salt Lake in 1953, carrying forward the fine traditions. In 1960, after Dingbian Saltern was decentralized to local government, Dingbian Salt Chemical Plant was established and gradually developed into a pillar enterprise of county economy. In 2001, Dingbian Salt Chemical Plant was transformed into Dingbian Changcheng Salt Chemical Co., Ltd. Through the efforts of several generations of people in Dingbian Saltern, the enterprise spirit of "working hard, pioneering and innovating" has been passed down from generation to generation. The National Industrial Heritage protection and utilization project centers on revolution-themed tours to the salt lake, which will bring new life and look to the salt lake.

贰：核心物项
Section two: Core items

陕甘宁边区政府集体食堂专用盐罐。
A special salt pot for the canteen of Shaan-Gan-Ning border region government.

陕甘宁边区政府当年使用的秤砣。
A steelyard used by the government of Shaan-Gan-Ning border region.

三五九旅盐湖拦洪坝遗址。
359 brigade salt lake flood dam site.

苟池盐湖及盐田，三五九旅打盐盐田和住宿遗址，三五九旅盐湖拦洪坝遗址，定边盐化厂办公楼遗址；盐罐（带陕甘宁边区定边盐场字样），秤砣（带陕甘边区盐场堡盐场字样）。

Gouchi salt lake and saltern, 359 brigade saltern and accommodation site, 359 brigade salt lake flood dam site, Dingbian Salt Chemical Plant office building site, salt pot (with the words of Dingbian Saltern in Shaan-Gan-Ning border region), and steelyard (with the words of Yanchangbu Saltern in Shaan-Gan border region).

陕西

国家工业遗产（第三批）

阅读链接 Link for further reading

定边盐湖打盐运动
Salt Production Movement in Dingbian Salt Lake

  1937年9月6日，陕甘宁边区政府宣告正式成立，陕甘宁边区的革命斗争自此进入了新的历史时期。为响应毛泽东主席"发展经济、保障供给、自力更生、丰衣足食"的伟大号召，1940年6月，八路军第一二〇师三五九旅2 000余名指战员在定边盐湖畔的长城上挖窑洞175孔，"割草铺地为床，垒土筑灶为炊"，同当地群众共同掀起了打盐大生产运动，解决了260余万边区抗日军民的食盐问题，同时为边区换回棉布、医药、钢铁、纸张和百货等大量急需物资，有力地支持了边区财政和抗日战争，被毛泽东主席誉为"中央第一财政"。

  On September 6th, 1937, the government of Shaan-Gan-Ning border region was officially established, and the revolution of Shaan-Gan-Ning border region entered a new historical period. In response to Chairman Mao Zedong's great call of "developing economy, ensuring supply, self-reliance and adequate food and clothing", in June 1940, more than 2 000 officers and men of 359 brigade of the 120th division of the Eighth Route Army dug 175 cave dwellings in the Great Wall by the Dingbian Salt Lake, "mowed grass and paved the ground for bed, built mud stoves for cooking". Together with the local people, they launched the Salt Production Movement, providing salt for more than 2.6 million Anti Japanese soldiers and civilians. Meanwhile, the salt was produced in exchange for a large number of much-needed supplies, such as cotton cloth, medicine, steel, paper and other daily needs, which strongly supported the finance of the border region and the War of Resistance Against Japan Aggression. It was praised as "the first governmentfinance contributor" by Chairman Mao Zedong.

三五九旅打盐大生产运动住宿遗址。
Accommodation site of the 359 brigade in Salt Production Movement.

七彩苟池盐田。
Colorful Gouchi Saltern.

定边盐湖群中最大的盐湖——苟池盐湖鸟瞰图。
An aerial view of Gouchi Salt Lake, the largest salt lake in Dingbian Salt Lake Group.

叁：遗产活化
Section three: Revitalization

定边盐湖群共有大小盐湖 14 个，湖盆面积 98 平方千米，目前已开采 7 个盐湖。为进一步挖掘定边盐场工业遗产的社会和经济价值，弘扬三五九旅"自力更生、不怕困难"的光荣传统和延长石油埋头苦干的企业精神，延长石油定边盐化工有限公司与政府共同投资 3.2 亿元，建设集自然风光、人文景观、革命历史教育为一体的红色盐都。

Dingbian Salt Lake Group has 14 salt lakes with a basin area of 98 square kilometers. At present, 7 salt lakes have been exploited. In order to further expend the social and economic value of the industrial heritage of Dingbian saltern, carry forward the glorious tradition of "self-reliance and no fear of difficulties" of 359 brigade, and Yanchang Petroleum's enterprise spirit of hard work, Yanchang Petroleum Dingbian Salt Chemical Industry Company and the government jointly invested 320 million yuan to build a red salt city integrating natural scenery, cultural landscape and revolutionary history education.

苟池盐湖新姿。
New appearance of Gouchi Salt Lake.

遗产名称/位置：定边盐场/陕西省榆林市定边县
Heritage item/Location: Dingbian Saltern/Dingbian County, Yulin City, Shaanxi Province

项目以盐为主题，包括繁荣的古盐市、激情盐景园、保健养生馆、盐湖特色小镇、三五九旅打盐遗址博物馆，分别对应印象盐雕、风情、欢乐等主题，总体规划2 200亩，从2019年3月到2023年3月分三期建设。目前，项目规划已经完成，正在进入实施阶段。

The salt-themed projects includes prosperous ancient salt city, passionate salt garden, health care center, characteristic town of salt lake and 359 Brigade Salt Relics Museum, which echo to the themes of impression salt carving, customs, and happiness. The overall plan of the project is 2 200 mu and will be constructed in three phases from March 2019 to March 2023. At the moment, the project planning has been finished and is entering the implementation stage.

三五九旅打盐大生产运动盐田遗址，部分已改造为红色旅游场所。
359 brigade saltern site of Salt Production Movement, part of which has already been transformed into a red tourist site.

陕西

国家工业遗产（第三批）

中核 504 厂

中国浓缩铀工业崛起之地
The Rising Place of China's Enriched Uranium Industry

壹：遗产春秋
Section one: History

1958年5月31日，时任中共中央总书记邓小平批准了中国第一座铀浓缩厂——中核504厂的选址方案。1964年1月，中核504厂取得首批合格产品，先后为我国第一颗原子弹、第一颗氢弹、第一艘核潜艇和第一座核电站提供了合格装料，实现了保家卫国的强军梦。

On May 31st, 1958, Deng Xiaoping, then the General Secretary of the Communist Party of China Central Committee, approved the site of China's first enriched uranium plant— China Nuclear Plant 504 in person. In January 1964, China Nuclear Plant 504 produced the first batch of qualified products. It provided qualified loading materials for China's first atomic bomb, first hydrogen bomb, first nuclear submarine and first nuclear power plant. It realized the dream of building a strong military and defending our country.

中核兰铀公司黄河铁桥，于1958年12月竣工使用，全长422米，其中主桥长度257.01米，是钢梁铁路、公路两用大桥，是中核兰铀公司与外界联系、进出物资材料和人员的重要通道，被兰铀人视为"功勋桥"。

Yellow River Iron Bridge of China Nuclear Lanzhou Enriched Uranium Company was completed in December 1958. The bridge is 422 meters long, with the main potoon 257.01 meters long. Functioning as both the steel-beam railway and highway, it is an important channel for China Nuclear Lanzhou Enriched Uranium Company to contact with the outside world, to transport cargo materials and commuting personnel. Thus it is deemed as "feat bridge" by its workers.

遗产名称/位置：中核504厂/甘肃省兰州市
Heritage item/Location: China Nuclear Plant 504 / Lanzhou City, Gansu Province

历经60余年的发展，中核504厂相继完成了第一个国产铀浓缩示范工程和第一个国产千吨级铀浓缩工程，为铀浓缩实现自主化、国产化和工业化应用发挥了独特作用，是目前国内规模最大的铀浓缩生产基地。

After over 60 years development, China Nuclear Plant 504 has completed the first domestic enriched uranium demonstration project and the first domestic thousand-ton-level enriched uranium project. The plant has played a unique role for the autonomy, localization and industrialization of uranium enrichment. It is currently the largest domestic enriched uranium production base.

贰：核心物项
Section two: Core items

邓小平留影处，工人俱乐部，河心泵站，黄河铁桥，老主工艺大厅遗址；国家科技进步奖一等奖奖牌、奖状（1978年）。

Photograph spot of Deng Xiaoping, Workers' Club, eyot pumping station, Yellow River Iron Bridge, relics of old main craft hall, the first prize medal and certificate of the National Science and Technology Progress Award (1978).

1964年4月12日，时任中共中央总书记的邓小平到中核504厂视察工作，并在厂区保健食堂前和大家合影留念，充分体现了党中央对核工业、对中核504厂的高度重视，激励着504人发奋图强、再创辉煌。图为保健食堂外景。

On April 12th, 1964, Deng Xiaoping, then the General Secretary of the Central Committee of Communist Party of China, came to China Nuclear Plant 504 for an inspection. He took a photo with workers in front of the healthy canteen. This fully reflected the central committee's high regard for nuclear industry and for China Nuclear Plant 504, and inspired its workers to work hard and to create new glory. The picture is the periphery of the healthy canteen.

国家工业遗产（第三批）

1961年8月开工建设，1964年9月交付使用的河心泵站，建筑面积992平方米，是中核兰铀公司在黄河取用生产、生活用水的主要取水口。

Eyot pumping station started construction in August 1961 and was put to use in September 1964. With a construction area of 992 square meters, it is the main water intake spot of China Nuclear Lanzhou Enriched Uranium Company for production and domestic water in the Yellow River.

老主工艺大厅于1963年12月交付使用。主要任务是采用气体扩散工艺技术进行铀同位素分离。大厅内有100余台机组、数千台主机组成的主工艺生产级联系统，先后为我国第一颗原子弹、第一颗氢弹、第一艘核潜艇、第一座核电站提供了核燃料，创造了中国核工业的"四个第一"。2000年12月31日，该大厅停止生产，图为恢复厂房修建前原貌。

Old main craft hall was put into use in December 1963. Its main task was to use gas diffusion technology to separate uranium isotope. There were more than 100 machinery sets and cascade system for main crafting production composed by thousands of main engines. It had provided qualified nuclear fuel for China's first atomic bomb, first hydrogen bomb, first nuclear submarine and first nuclear power plant and had created "four first" in China's nuclear industry. On 31st December 2000, the old main craft hall stopped production. The picture shows the original condition of the factory before renovated.

遗产名称 / 位置：中核 504 厂 / 甘肃省兰州市
Heritage item/Location: China Nuclear Plant 504 / Lanzhou City, Gansu Province

叁：遗产今夕
Section three: Current Situation

近年来，遗产核心物项的保护工作逐步展开，包括加固、电气系统改造、防水、内部装修等。针对在服役过程中曾为"两弹一艇"事业做出了突出贡献的我国第一座核反应堆，在完成阶段性退役工作后，中核兰州铀浓缩有限公司将采取相关保护措施，使之成为传承核工业精神及军工文化的重要阵地。

In recent years, the protection of the core heritage items has been gradually carried out, including reinforcement, electrical system transformation, waterproofing, interior decoration and so on. As to China's first nuclear reactor, which has made an outstanding contribution made to the cause of "two bombs and one nuclear submarine", China Nuclear Lanzhou Enriched Uranium Company will take relevant protection measures to make it an important spot to pass on the spirit of the nuclear industry and military culture after some phase of decommissioning work.

工人俱乐部是中核504厂在建设初期为丰富职工生活、召开各类会议而兴建的大型苏式礼堂，于1962年10月建成交付使用，建筑面积6 036平方米，内设1 212个座位、舞台、图书馆、棋牌室、练功房、电影放映室、会议室等，是孕育、发展、创新和丰富中核504厂企业文化、展现兰铀人良好精神风貌与核工业精神的标志性建筑。

The Workers' Club was a large-scale Soviet-style auditorium building constructed in the early days by China Nuclear Plant 504 to enrich the amateur cultural life of its employees and to hold various meetings. With a construction area of 6 036 square meters and 1 212 seats, it was put into use in October 1962. The Worker's Club consisted of stage, library, chess room, dance studio, film screening room and conference room. It was a landmark building that bred, developed, created and enriched corporate culture of China Nuclear Plant 504 and that reflected the high spirit of China Nuclear Lanzhou Enriched Uranium Company's workers and that of nuclear industry.